I0028630

Debugging.TV Frames

10-year Anniversary Edition
Est. October 2011

Test Windows Error Reporting

☐ Software Exception   ☐ Handled Exception

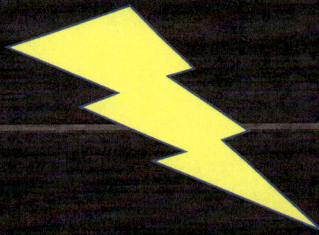

TestWER.exe.2356.dmp

10000011 11000100 00000100 11000010 00010100 00000000 10010000 10111000
01011001 00000000 00000000 00000000 00110011 11001001 10001101 01010100
00100100 00000100 01100100 11111111 00010101 11000000 00000000 00000000
00000000 10000011 11000100 00000100 11000010 00010000 00000000 10111000
01011010 00000000 00000000 00000000 00110011 11001001 10001101 01010100
00100100 00000100 01100100 11111111 00010101 11000000 00000000 00000000
00000000 10000011 11000100 00000100 11000010 00001000 00000000 10111000
01011011 00000000 00000000 00000000 00110011 11001001 10001101 01010100
00100100 00000100 01100100 11111111 00010101 11000000 00000000 00000000
00000000 10000011 11000100 00000100 11000010 00010000 00000000 10111000
01011100 00000000 00000000 00000000 00110011 11001001 10001101 01010100
00100100 00000100 01100100 11111111 00010101 11000000 00000000 00000000
00000000 10000011 11000100 00000100 11000010 00010100 00000000 10111000
01011101 00000000 00000000 00000000 00110011 11001001 10001101 01010100
00100100 00000100 01100100 11111111 00010101 11000000 00000000 00000000
00000000 10000011 11000100 00000100 11000010 00011000 00000000 10111000
01011110 00000000 00000000 00000000 10111001 00000111 00000000 00000000
00000000 10001101 01010100 00100100 00000100 01100100 11111111 00010101

http://support.citrix.com/article/CTX111901

Σψμβολσ

```
0:000> k

ChildEBP RetAddr
WARNING: Stack unwind information not available. Following frames may be wrong.
0018f234 76ce162d ntdll!NtWaitForMultipleObjects+0x15
0018f27c 76ce1921 kernel32!WaitForMultipleObjectsEx+0x8e
0018f298 76d09b2d kernel32!WaitForMultipleObjects+0x18
0018f304 76d09bca kernel32!CheckForReadOnlyResource+0x175
0018f318 76d098f8 kernel32!CheckForReadOnlyResource+0x212
0018f328 76d09875 kernel32!UnhandledExceptionFilter+0x163
0018f3b4 77bc0df7 kernel32!UnhandledExceptionFilter+0xe0
0018ffd4 77b89ed5 ntdll!RtlKnownExceptionFilter+0xb7
0018ffec 00000000 ntdll!RtlInitializeExceptionChain+0x36

0:000> !teb
TEB at 7efdd000
*********************************************************************
***                                                              ***
***                                                              ***
***      Your debugger is not using the correct symbols          ***
***                                                              ***
***      In order for this command to work properly, your symbol path  ***
***      must point to .pdb files that have full type information.  ***
***                                                              ***
***      Certain .pdb files (such as the public OS symbols) do not  ***
***      contain the required information.  Contact the group that  ***
***      provided you with these symbols if you need this command to  ***
***      work.                                                    ***
***                                                              ***
***      Type referenced: nt!_TEB                                ***
***                                                              ***
*********************************************************************
error InitTypeRead( TEB )...
```

```
Symbols from PE tables:

...
symbolA                     address1
symbolB                     address2
CheckForReadOnlyResource    76d099b8
...


0:000> X kernel32!CheckForReadOnlyResource
76d099b8 kernel32!CheckForReadOnlyResource
(<no parameter info>)

0:000> ? 76d099b8+175
Evaluate expression: 1993382701 = 76d09b2d

0:000> ln 76d09b2d
(76d099b8)
kernel32!CheckForReadOnlyResource+0x175   |
(76d09daa)
kernel32!GetThreadSelectorEntry
```

Symβολσ

```
0:000> .symfix c:\mss

0:000> .reload
...................
0:000> k
ChildEBP RetAddr
0018f198 75670bdd ntdll!NtWaitForMultipleObjects+0x15
0018f234 76ce162d KERNELBASE!WaitForMultipleObjectsEx+0x100
0018f27c 76ce1921 kernel32!WaitForMultipleObjectsExImplementation+0xe0
0018f298 76d09b2d kernel32!WaitForMultipleObjects+0x18
0018f304 76d09bca kernel32!WerpReportFaultInternal+0x186
0018f318 76d098f8 kernel32!WerpReportFault+0x70
0018f328 76d09875 kernel32!BasepReportFault+0x20
0018f3b4 77bc0df7 kernel32!UnhandledExceptionFilter+0x1af
0018f3bc 77bc0cd4 ntdll!__RtlUserThreadStart+0x62
0018f3d0 77bc0b71 ntdll!_EH4_CallFilterFunc+0x12
0018f3f8 77b96ac9 ntdll!_except_handler4+0x8e
0018f41c 77b96a9b ntdll!ExecuteHandler2+0x26
0018f4cc 77b6010f ntdll!ExecuteHandler+0x24
0018f4cc 0041ff21 ntdll!KiUserExceptionDispatcher+0xf
*** ERROR: Module load completed but symbols could not be loaded for TestWER.exe
WARNING: Stack unwind information not available. Following frames may be wrong.
0018f850 00403620 TestWER+0x1ff21
0018f860 0040382f TestWER+0x3620
0018f890 00402df6 TestWER+0x382f
0018f8b4 00409ef8 TestWER+0x2df6
[...]
0018ff88 76ce3677 TestWER+0xfc3e
0018ff94 77b89f02 kernel32!BaseThreadInitThunk+0xe
0018ffd4 77b89ed5 ntdll!__RtlUserThreadStart+0x70
0018ffec 00000000 ntdll!_RtlUserThreadStart+0x1b
```

```
Compare before and after MSS:

0:000> X kernel32!*
[...]
0:000> .symfix c:\mss

0:000> .reload
...................
0:000> X kernel32!*
[...]
```

Symbols

```
0:000> .sympath+ C:\TestWER\x86
Symbol search path is: srv*;C:\TestWER\x86
Expanded Symbol search path is: SRV*c:\mss*http://msdl.microsoft.com/download/symbols;c:\testwer\x86

0:000> .reload
......................

0:000> kL
ChildEBP RetAddr
0018f198 75670bdd ntdll!NtWaitForMultipleObjects+0x15
0018f234 76ce162d KERNELBASE!WaitForMultipleObjectsEx+0x100
0018f27c 76ce1921 kernel32!WaitForMultipleObjectsExImplementation+0xe0
0018f298 76d09b2d kernel32!WaitForMultipleObjects+0x18
0018f304 76d09bca kernel32!WerpReportFaultInternal+0x186
0018f318 76d098f8 kernel32!WerpReportFault+0x70
0018f328 76d09875 kernel32!BasepReportFault+0x20
0018f3b4 77bc0df7 kernel32!UnhandledExceptionFilter+0x1af
0018f3bc 77bc0cd4 ntdll!__RtlUserThreadStart+0x62
0018f3d0 77bc0b71 ntdll!_EH4_CallFilterFunc+0x12
0018f3f8 77b96ac9 ntdll!_except_handler4+0x8e
0018f41c 77b96a9b ntdll!ExecuteHandler2+0x26
0018f4cc 77b6010f ntdll!ExecuteHandler+0x24
0018f4cc 0041ff21 ntdll!KiUserExceptionDispatcher+0xf
0018f850 00403620 TestWER!CTestDefaultDebuggerDlg::OnBnClickedButton1+0xb1
0018f860 0040382f TestWER!_AfxDispatchCmdMsg+0x45
0018f890 00402df6 TestWER!CCmdTarget::OnCmdMsg+0x11c
0018f8b4 00409ef8 TestWER!CDialog::OnCmdMsg+0x1d
[...]
0018ff88 76ce3677 TestWER!__tmainCRTStartup+0x112
0018ff94 77b89f02 kernel32!BaseThreadInitThunk+0xe
0018ffd4 77b89ed5 ntdll!__RtlUserThreadStart+0x70
0018ffec 00000000 ntdll!_RtlUserThreadStart+0x1b
```

```
Compare before and after loading
TestWER PDB file:

0:000> X TestWER!*
[...]

0:000> .sympath+ C:\TestWER\x86
0:000> .reload
......................
0:000> X TestWER!*
[...]
```

Symβols

```
0:000> !teb
TEB at 7efdd000
    ExceptionList:        0018f224
    StackBase:            00190000
    StackLimit:           0018d000
[...]

0:000> dps 0018d000 00190000
0018d000  00000000
[...]
0018deec  00000000
0018def0  7524a010 CRYPTBASE!g_AesCtrSafeCtx+0x924
0018def4  0018df0c
[...]
0018df04  0018df24
0018df08  77b7fa19 ntdll!LdrpFindLoadedDllByName+0x68
0018df0c  0018e004
[...]

0:000> ub 7524a010
CRYPTBASE!g_AesCtrSafeCtx+0x914:
7524a000 0000            add     byte ptr [eax],al
7524a002 0000            add     byte ptr [eax],al
7524a004 0000            add     byte ptr [eax],al
7524a006 0000            add     byte ptr [eax],al

0:000> ub 77b7fa19
ntdll!LdrpFindLoadedDllByName+0x77:
[...]
77b7fa10 50              push    eax
77b7fa11 ff7508          push    dword ptr [ebp+8]
77b7fa14 e8faedffff      call    ntdll!RtlEqualUnicodeString (77b7e813)
```

```
* ASCII or UNICODE fragments *
[...]
0018f6f4  00000000
0018f6f8  00000000
0018f6fc  00000000
0018f700  9f43baaa
0018f704  678f805c
0018f708  00010010
0018f70c  00000000
0018f710  006f0043
0018f714  00720072
0018f718  00630065
0018f71c  00690074
0018f720  00000000
0018f724  00000000
[...]

0:000> du 0018f710
0018f710  "Correcti"
```

Patterns

No Component Symbols

Coincidental Symbolic Information

Incorrect Symbolic Information

Debugging.TV

Frame 0x02

Presenter: Dmitry Vostokov

MEMORY DUMP ANALYSIS SERVICES

DumpAnalysis.com

Including Crash and Hang Analysis Audit, Training and Seminars

Sponsors

OPENTASK
Iterative and Incremental Publishing

Troubleshooting Symbols

© 2011 DumpAnalysis.org + TraceAnalysis.org

App Version 1

```
0:000> .sympath+ C:\DebuggingTV\DebuggingTV02\x64\Release\Version1

0:000> .reload
..............

0:000> kL
Child-SP          RetAddr           Call Site
00000000`001cfb38 00000000`76e7e6fa user32!ZwUserGetMessage+0xa
00000000`001cfb40 00000001`3fa610d0 user32!GetMessageW+0x34
00000000`001cfb70 00000001`3fa61494 DebuggingTV02!wWinMain+0xd0
00000000`001cfbd0 00000000`76d5cdcd DebuggingTV02!__tmainCRTStartup+0x154
00000000`001cfc80 00000000`76f7c6e1 kernel32!BaseThreadInitThunk+0xd
00000000`001cfcb0 00000000`00000000 ntdll!RtlUserThreadStart+0x1d

0:000> ub 00000001`3fa610d0
DebuggingTV02!wWinMain+0xac [c:\debuggingtv\debuggingtv02\debuggingtv02\debuggingtv02.cpp @ 50]:
00000001`3fa610ac call    qword ptr [DebuggingTV02!_imp_TranslateMessage (00000001`3fa66228)]
00000001`3fa610b2 lea     rcx,[rsp+20h]
00000001`3fa610b7 call    qword ptr [DebuggingTV02!_imp_DispatchMessageW (00000001`3fa66220)]
00000001`3fa610bd lea     rcx,[rsp+20h]
00000001`3fa610c2 xor     r9d,r9d
00000001`3fa610c5 xor     r8d,r8d
00000001`3fa610c8 xor     edx,edx
00000001`3fa610ca call    qword ptr [DebuggingTV02!_imp_GetMessageW (00000001`3fa66238)]
```

© 2011 DumpAnalysis.org + TraceAnalysis.org

App Version 2

```
0:000> .sympath+ C:\DebuggingTV\DebuggingTV02\x64\Release\Version1

0:000> .reload

0:000> kL
Child-SP          RetAddr           Call Site
00000000`001dfa88 00000000`76e7e6fa user32!ZwUserGetMessage+0xa
*** ERROR: Module load completed but symbols could not be loaded for DebuggingTV02.exe
00000000`001dfa90 00000001`3f3f10d0 user32!GetMessageW+0x34
00000000`001dfac0 00000001`3f3f1494 DebuggingTV02+0x10d0
00000000`001dfb20 00000000`76d5cdcd DebuggingTV02+0x1494
00000000`001dfbd0 00000000`76f7c6e1 kernel32!BaseThreadInitThunk+0xd
00000000`001dfc00 00000000`00000000 ntdll!RtlUserThreadStart+0x1d

0:000> .reload /f /i DebuggingTV02.exe

0:000> kL
Child-SP          RetAddr           Call Site
00000000`001dfa88 00000000`76e7e6fa user32!ZwUserGetMessage+0xa
00000000`001dfa90 00000001`3f3f10d0 user32!GetMessageW+0x34
00000000`001dfac0 00000001`3f3f1494 DebuggingTV02!wWinMain+0xd0
00000000`001dfb20 00000000`76d5cdcd DebuggingTV02!__tmainCRTStartup+0x154
00000000`001dfbd0 00000000`76f7c6e1 kernel32!BaseThreadInitThunk+0xd
00000000`001dfc00 00000000`00000000 ntdll!RtlUserThreadStart+0x1d
```

© 2011 DumpAnalysis.org + TraceAnalysis.org

...continue

```
0:000> .asm no_code_bytes
Assembly options: no_code_bytes



0:000> ub 00000001`3f3f10d0
DebuggingTV02!wWinMain+0xac [c:\debuggingtv\debuggingtv02\debuggingtv02\debuggingtv02.cpp @ 50]:
00000001`3f3f10ac call    qword ptr [DebuggingTV02!_imp_TranslateMessage (00000001`3f3f6228)]
00000001`3f3f10b2 lea     rcx,[rsp+20h]
00000001`3f3f10b7 call    qword ptr [DebuggingTV02!_imp_DispatchMessageW (00000001`3f3f6220)]
00000001`3f3f10bd lea     rcx,[rsp+20h]
00000001`3f3f10c2 xor     r9d,r9d
00000001`3f3f10c5 xor     r8d,r8d
00000001`3f3f10c8 xor     edx,edx
00000001`3f3f10ca call    qword ptr [DebuggingTV02!_imp_GetMessageW (00000001`3f3f6238)]


0:000> ub 00000001`3f3f1494
DebuggingTV02!__tmainCRTStartup+0x133 [f:\dd\vctools\crt_bld\self_64_amd64\crt\src\crt0.c @ 275]:
00000001`3f3f1473 test    byte ptr [rsp+6Ch],1
00000001`3f3f1478 movzx   edx,word ptr [rsp+70h]
00000001`3f3f147d mov     r9d,0Ah
00000001`3f3f1483 cmovne  r9d,edx
00000001`3f3f1487 mov     r8,rax
00000001`3f3f148a xor     edx,edx
00000001`3f3f148c mov     rcx,rdi
00000001`3f3f148f call    DebuggingTV02!wWinMain (00000001`3f3f1000)
```

© 2011 DumpAnalysis.org + TraceAnalysis.org

App Version 4

```
0:000> .sympath+ C:\DebuggingTV\DebuggingTV02\Release\Version1

0:000> .reload

0:000> .reload /f /i DebuggingTV02.exe

0:000> kL
ChildEBP RetAddr
001bf968 7675199a ntdll!KiFastSystemCallRet
001bf96c 767519cd user32!NtUserGetMessage+0xc
001bf988 003f1045 user32!GetMessageW+0x33
001bf9a8 003f10f2 DebuggingTV02!wWinMain+0x45
001bf9ac 031f0197 DebuggingTV02!MyRegisterClass+0x2
WARNING: Frame IP not in any known module. Following frames may be wrong.
001bf9d8 003f141d 0x31f0197
001bfa3c 003f2914 DebuggingTV02!__tmainCRTStartup+0x139
001bfa68 76573833 DebuggingTV02!__security_init_cookie+0x85
001bfa74 77c1a9bd kernel32!BaseThreadInitThunk+0xe
001bfab4 00000000 ntdll!_RtlUserThreadStart+0x23


0:000> ub 031f0197
                ^ Unable to find valid previous instruction for 'ub 031f0197'
```

© 2011 DumpAnalysis.org + TraceAnalysis.org

...continue

```
0:000> .sympath+ C:\DebuggingTV\DebuggingTV02\Release\Version4

0:000> .reload

0:000> kL
ChildEBP RetAddr
001bf968 7675199a ntdll!KiFastSystemCallRet
001bf96c 767519cd user32!NtUserGetMessage+0xc
001bf988 003f1045 user32!GetMessageW+0x33
001bf9a8 003f10f2 DebuggingTV02!MessageLoop+0x45
001bf9d8 003f141d DebuggingTV02!wWinMain+0xa2
001bfa68 76573833 DebuggingTV02!__tmainCRTStartup+0x11a
001bfa74 77c1a9bd kernel32!BaseThreadInitThunk+0xe
001bfab4 00000000 ntdll!_RtlUserThreadStart+0x23
```

© 2011 DumpAnalysis.org + TraceAnalysis.org

Troubleshooting Symbols

© 2011 DumpAnalysis.org + TraceAnalysis.org

Symbol Problem

```
0:000> k

ChildEBP RetAddr
WARNING: Stack unwind information not available. Following frames may be wrong.
0018f234 76ce162d ntdll!NtWaitForMultipleObjects+0x15
0018f27c 76ce1921 kernel32!WaitForMultipleObjectsEx+0x8e
0018f298 76d09b2d kernel32!WaitForMultipleObjects+0x18
0018f304 76d09bca kernel32!CheckForReadOnlyResource+0x175
0018f318 76d098f8 kernel32!CheckForReadOnlyResource+0x212
0018f328 76d09875 kernel32!UnhandledExceptionFilter+0x163
0018f3b4 77bc0df7 kernel32!UnhandledExceptionFilter+0xe0
0018ffd4 77b89ed5 ntdll!RtlKnownExceptionFilter+0xb7
0018ffec 00000000 ntdll!RtlInitializeExceptionChain+0x36


0:000> .symfix c:\mss


0:000> .reload
......................
*** ERROR: Symbol file could not be found.  Defaulted to export symbols for ntdll.dll -
```

© 2011 DumpAnalysis.org + TraceAnalysis.org

Bad Trace

```
0:000> k

ChildEBP RetAddr
WARNING: Stack unwind information not available. Following frames may be wrong.
0018f234 76ce162d ntdll!NtWaitForMultipleObjects+0x15
0018f27c 76ce1921 kernel32!WaitForMultipleObjectsExImplementation+0xe0
0018f298 76d09b2d kernel32!WaitForMultipleObjects+0x18
0018f304 76d09bca kernel32!WerpReportFaultInternal+0x186
0018f318 76d098f8 kernel32!WerpReportFault+0x70
0018f328 76d09875 kernel32!BasepReportFault+0x20
0018f3b4 77bc0df7 kernel32!UnhandledExceptionFilter+0x1af
0018ffd4 77b89ed5 ntdll!RtlKnownExceptionFilter+0xb7
0018ffec 00000000 ntdll!RtlInitializeExceptionChain+0x36
```

© 2011 DumpAnalysis.org + TraceAnalysis.org

Symbol Tracing

```
0:000> !sym noisy
noisy mode - symbol prompts on


0:000> .reload
.......................

SYMSRV:  c:\mss\wntdll.pdb\FC9DB05873374DB5985BABAA3F8F734F2\wntdll.pd_
         The file or directory is corrupted and unreadable.
DBGHELP: wntdll.pdb - file not found
*** ERROR: Symbol file could not be found.  Defaulted to export symbols for ntdll.dll -
DBGHELP: ntdll - export symbols
```

© 2011 DumpAnalysis.org + TraceAnalysis.org

Symbol Fix

```
C:\mss\wntdll.pdb\FC9DB05873374DB5985BABAA3F8F734F2>expand wntdll.pd_ wntdll.pdb

Microsoft (R) File Expansion Utility  Version 6.1.7600.16385
Copyright (c) Microsoft Corporation. All rights reserved.


Copying wntdll.pd_ to wntdll.pdb.
wntdll.pd_: 2124800 bytes copied.



C:\mss\wntdll.pdb\FC9DB05873374DB5985BABAA3F8F734F2>
```

```
0:000> .reload
......................
DBGHELP: ntdll - public symbols
        c:\mss\wntdll.pdb\FC9DB05873374DB5985BABAA3F8F734F2\wntdll.pdb
```

© 2011 DumpAnalysis.org + TraceAnalysis.org

Good Trace

```
0:000> !sym quiet
quiet mode - symbol prompts on


0:000> k
ChildEBP RetAddr
0018f198 75670bdd ntdll!NtWaitForMultipleObjects+0x15
0018f234 76ce162d KERNELBASE!WaitForMultipleObjectsEx+0x100
0018f27c 76ce1921 kernel32!WaitForMultipleObjectsExImplementation+0xe0
0018f298 76d09b2d kernel32!WaitForMultipleObjects+0x18
0018f304 76d09bca kernel32!WerpReportFaultInternal+0x186
0018f318 76d098f8 kernel32!WerpReportFault+0x70
0018f328 76d09875 kernel32!BasepReportFault+0x20
0018f3b4 77bc0df7 kernel32!UnhandledExceptionFilter+0x1af
0018f3bc 77bc0cd4 ntdll!__RtlUserThreadStart+0x62
0018f3d0 77bc0b71 ntdll!_EH4_CallFilterFunc+0x12
0018f3f8 77b96ac9 ntdll!_except_handler4+0x8e
0018f41c 77b96a9b ntdll!ExecuteHandler2+0x26
0018f4cc 77b6010f ntdll!ExecuteHandler+0x24
0018f4cc 0041ff21 ntdll!KiUserExceptionDispatcher+0xf
[...]
```

© 2011 DumpAnalysis.org + TraceAnalysis.org

Debugging.TV

Frame 0x04

Presenter: Dmitry Vostokov

MEMORY DUMP ANALYSIS SERVICES

DumpAnalysis.com

Including Crash and Hang Analysis Audit, Training and Seminars

Sponsors

OPENTASK
Iterative and Incremental Publishing

Debugging
Improvisation
0x01

© 2011 DumpAnalysis.org + TraceAnalysis.org

Topics

- Invasive and noninvasive debugging
- Suspended threads
- Stack trace and symbols
- TEB and raw stack
- Breakpoints
- Detaching and attaching
- Breaking in
- Saving dump files
- Creating CAB file

© 2011 DumpAnalysis.org + TraceAnalysis.org

Commands

~	bc	bl
k	.detach	lm
!teb	.attach	bp
dps	g	.symopt
.symfix	.dump	~n
.reload	.opendump	~m
	.dumpcab	

© 2011 DumpAnalysis.org + TraceAnalysis.org

Debugging.TV

Frame 0x05

Presenter: Dmitry Vostokov

MEMORY DUMP ANALYSIS SERVICES

DumpAnalysis.com

Including Crash and Hang Analysis Audit, Training and Seminars

Sponsors

OPENTASK
Iterative and Incremental Publishing

Debugging Improvisation 0x02

© 2011 DumpAnalysis.org + TraceAnalysis.org

Topics

- Software breakpoints
- Software breakpoint implementation
- Hardware breakpoints
- Debug registers
- !Ad

© 2011 DumpAnalysis.org + TraceAnalysis.org

Commands

.logopen   bp

kL   u

.reload   bc

~<>s   bl

x   .bpcmds

.symfix   ~

.sympath   Ba

rM   uf

© 2011 DumpAnalysis.org + TraceAnalysis.org

Software Breakpoint

© 2011 DumpAnalysis.org + TraceAnalysis.org

```
0:000> * Debugger View

0:000> u TestWER64!CAboutDlg::CAboutDlg
TestWER64!CAboutDlg::CAboutDlg:
00000001`400249d0 48894c2408      mov     qword ptr [rsp+8],rcx
00000001`400249d5 4883ec38        sub     rsp,38h
00000001`400249d9 48c7442420feffffff mov   qword ptr [rsp+20h],0FFFFFFFFFFFFFFFEh
00000001`400249e2 4533c0          xor     r8d,r8d
00000001`400249e5 ba64000000      mov     edx,64h
00000001`400249ea 488b4c2440      mov     rcx,qword ptr [rsp+40h]
00000001`400249ef e844e9fdff      call    TestWER64!CDialog::CDialog (00000001`40003338)
00000001`400249f4 90              nop


0:000> * Another Debugger View

0:000> u TestWER64!CAboutDlg::CAboutDlg
TestWER64!CAboutDlg::CAboutDlg:
00000001`400249d0 cc              int     3
00000001`400249d1 894c2408        mov     dword ptr [rsp+8],ecx
00000001`400249d5 4883ec38        sub     rsp,38h
00000001`400249d9 48c7442420feffffff mov   qword ptr [rsp+20h],0FFFFFFFFFFFFFFFEh
00000001`400249e2 4533c0          xor     r8d,r8d
00000001`400249e5 ba64000000      mov     edx,64h
00000001`400249ea 488b4c2440      mov     rcx,qword ptr [rsp+40h]
00000001`400249ef e844e9fdff      call    TestWER64!CDialog::CDialog (00000001`40003338)
```

Hardware Breakpoint

```
0:000> rM20
dr0=0000000000000000 dr1=0000000000000000 dr2=0000000000000000
dr3=0000000000000000 dr6=0000000000000000 dr7=0000000000000000
USER32!NtUserGetMessage+0xa:
00000000`774dc92a c3              ret


0:000> ba e 1 TestWER64!CAboutDlg::CAboutDlg


0:000> bl
 0 e 00000001`400249d0 e 1 0001 (0001)  0:**** TestWER64!CAboutDlg::CAboutDlg


0:000> g
(5e0.140): Break instruction exception - code 80000003 (first chance)
ntdll!DbgBreakPoint:
00000000`7760e910 cc              int     3


0:001> rM20
dr0=00000001400249d0 dr1=0000000000000000 dr2=0000000000000000
dr3=0000000000000000 dr6=00000000ffff0ff0 dr7=0000000000000401
ntdll!DbgBreakPoint:
00000000`7760e910 cc              int     3
```

© 2011 DumpAnalysis.org + TraceAnalysis.org

Debugging.TV

Frame 0x06

Presenter: Dmitry Vostokov

MEMORY DUMP ANALYSIS SERVICES

DumpAnalysis.com

Including Crash and Hang Analysis Audit, Training and Seminars

Sponsors

OPENTASK
Iterative and Incremental Publishing

Topics

- Value passing and register reuse
- Breakpoint execution commands
- WinDbg pseudo-registers and scripting
- Passing data between breakpoints
- Platform independent commands
- Logging window messages
- Module load events

© 2012 DumpAnalysis.org + TraceAnalysis.org

GetMessage

```
BOOL WINAPI GetMessage
(
__out LPMSG lpMsg,                  // RCX
__in_opt HWND hWnd,                 // RDX
__in UINT wMsgFilterMin,            // R8d
__in UINT wMsgFilterMax             // R9d
);
```

© 2012 DumpAnalysis.org + TraceAnalysis.org

MSG

```
typedef struct tagMSG {
    HWND    hwnd;              // 64
    UINT    message;          // 64
    WPARAM  wParam;           // 64
    LPARAM  lParam;           // 64
    DWORD   time;             // 32
    POINT   pt;               // 32, 32
} MSG, *PMSG, *LPMSG;
```

© 2012 DumpAnalysis.org + TraceAnalysis.org

Event State Management

```
0:000> ub 00000000`ff2d1064
notepad!WinMain+0xf5:
[...]
00000000`ff2d1051 488d4c2440      lea     rcx,[rsp+40h]           * bp 0
00000000`ff2d1056 4533c9          xor     r9d,r9d
00000000`ff2d1059 4533c0          xor     r8d,r8d
00000000`ff2d105c 33d2            xor     edx,edx
00000000`ff2d105e ff1524b40000    call    qword ptr [notepad!_imp_GetMessageW
(00000000`ff2dc488)]


0:000> u 00000000`ff2d1064
notepad!WinMain+0x182:
00000000`ff2d1064 413bc4          cmp     eax,r12d                * bp 1
00000000`ff2d1067 0f84b2060000    je      notepad!WinMain+0x18b (00000000`ff2d171f)
[...]


0:000> bl
 0 e 00000000`ff2d105e     0001 (0001)  0:**** notepad!WinMain+0x17c "r $t0 = rcx; g"
 1 e 00000000`ff2d1064     0001 (0001)  0:**** notepad!WinMain+0x182 ".printf \"hwnd: %p message:
%p wParam: %p lParam: %p\", poi(@$t0), poi(@$t0+@$ptrsize), poi(@$t0+2*@$ptrsize),
poi(@$t0+3*@$ptrsize); .echo; g"
```

© 2012 DumpAnalysis.org + TraceAnalysis.org

Commands and pseudo-registers

.logopen
kv
u
ub
bp
bl
g
r
dp

.printf
.echo
poi
$t0
$ptrsize
bc
dd
.logclose

© 2012 DumpAnalysis.org + TraceAnalysis.org

Topics

- Detecting corruption in executable modules
- Aliases
- Image paths
- Troubleshoting image path problems
- When we need image paths?

© 2012 DumpAnalysis.org + TraceAnalysis.org

Checking an Image

```
1: kd> !chkimg -d -v nt
Searching for module with expression: nt
Unable to open image file: C:\Program Files (x86)\Debugging Tools for Windows
(x86)\sym\ntkrpamp.exe\4549AE003a1000\ntkrpamp.exe
The system cannot find the file specified.

Error for nt: Could not find image file for the module. Make sure binaries are included in the symbol path.


1: kd> .sympath
Symbol search path is: srv*
Expanded Symbol search path is: SRV*c:\mss*http://msdl.microsoft.com/download/symbols


1: kd> .exepath+ SRV*c:\mss*http://msdl.microsoft.com/download/symbols
Executable image search path is: SRV*c:\mss*http://msdl.microsoft.com/download/symbols
Expanded Executable image search path is: srv*c:\mss*http://msdl.microsoft.com/download/symbols


1: kd> !chkimg -d -v nt
[...]
Scanning section:    .text
Size: 936109
Range to scan: 81801000-818e58ad
    81854019 - nt!PsGetCurrentProcess
            [ 64:24 ]
Total bytes compared: 936109(100%)
Number of errors: 1
[...]
```

© 2012 DumpAnalysis.org + TraceAnalysis.org

Aliases

```
1: kd> !for_each_module al
   Alias                Value
   -------              -------
   $CurrentDumpArchiveFile
   $CurrentDumpArchivePath
   $CurrentDumpFile K:\AWMDA-Dumps\32-bit\Kernel\MEMORY-CodeOverwrite.DMP
   $CurrentDumpPath K:\AWMDA-Dumps\32-bit\Kernel
   $lowrite             C:\Users\Administrator\AppData\Local\Temp\Low
   $ntdllnsym
   $ntdllsym
   $ntdllwsym
   $ntnsym              nt
   $ntsym               nt
   $ntwsym
   $tmpwrite            C:\Users\ADMINI~1\AppData\Local\Temp
   @#Base               80200000
   @#Checksum           0000a38f
   @#End                8020a000
   @#FileDescription
   @#FileVersion
   @#Flags              00000004
   @#ImageName          \SystemRoot\system32\DRIVERS\BATTC.SYS
   @#ImageNameSize  00000027
   @#LoadedImageName
   @#LoadedImageNameSize 00000001
   @#MappedImageName
   @#MappedImageNameSize 00000001
   @#ModuleIndex    00
   @#ModuleName         BATTC
   @#ModuleNameSize 00000006
   @#ProductVersion
   @#Size               0000a000
   @#SymbolFileName BATTC.SYS
   @#SymbolFileNameSize 0000000a
   @#SymbolType     5
   @#TimeDateStamp  4549adb4
[...]
```

© 2012 DumpAnalysis.org + TraceAnalysis.org

Checking All Modules

```
1: kd> !for_each_module -d -v @#ModuleName

[...]

Searching for module with expression: nt
Will apply relocation fixups to file used for comparison
Will ignore NOP/LOCK errors
Will ignore patched instructions
Image specific ignores will be applied
Comparison image path: C:\Program Files (x86)\Debugging Tools for Windows (x86)\sym\ntkrpamp.exe\4549AE003a1000\ntkrpamp.exe
No range specified


Scanning section:    .text
Size: 936109
Range to scan: 81801000-818e58ad
    81854019 - nt!PsGetCurrentProcess
            [ 64:24 ]
Total bytes compared: 936109(100%)
Number of errors: 1


[...]
```

© 2012 DumpAnalysis.org + TraceAnalysis.org

Commands and Aliases

.exepath   !chkimg

!for_each_module   @#ModuleName

al   .sympath

© 2012 DumpAnalysis.org + TraceAnalysis.org

Topics

- Logging WinDbg extension
- Adding your API for logging
- Different logging formats
- Viewing verbose logging extension logs

Tracing Win32 API while debugging a process

Activation Context pattern

© 2012 DumpAnalysis.org + TraceAnalysis.org

Custom Logging

C:\Program Files\Debugging Tools for Windows (x64)\winext\manifest\contexts.h

```
// ++++++++++++++++++++++++++++++++++++++++++++++++++++++++++++++++++++++++++++++++
//
//                         Activation Context API
//
// ++++++++++++++++++++++++++++++++++++++++++++++++++++++++++++++++++++++++++++++++
category ActivationContext:
module KERNEL32.DLL:
FailOnFalse ActivateActCtx(HANDLE hActCtx, [out] PULONG_PTR lpCookie);
FailOnFalse DeactivateActCtx(DWORD dwFlags, ULONG_PTR upCookie);
```

C:\Program Files\Debugging Tools for Windows (x64)\winext\manifest\main.h

```
[...]
#include "contexts.h"
```

© 2012 DumpAnalysis.org + TraceAnalysis.org

Enabling Logging

```
0:001> !logexts.loge

Windows API Logging Extensions  v3.01
Parsing the manifest files...
Location: C:\Program Files\Debugging Tools for Windows (x64)\winext\manifest\main.h
    Parsing file "main.h" ...
    Parsing file "winerror.h" ...
    Parsing file "kernel32.h" ...
[...]
Parsing completed.
Logexts injected. Output: "C:\Users\Training\Desktop\LogExts\"
Logging enabled.


0:001> !logc d *
All categories disabled.


0:001> !logc
Categories:

    1 ActivationContext              Disabled
    2 AdvApi32                       Disabled
[...]


0:001> !logc e 1
    1 ActivationContext              Enabled
```

© 2012 DumpAnalysis.org + TraceAnalysis.org

Logging Output

```
0:001> !logo
Logging currently enabled.

Output directory: C:\Users\Dump Analysis\Desktop\LogExts\

Output settings:
   Debugger           Disabled
   Text file          Disabled
   Verbose log        Enabled


0:001> !logo e t
   Debugger           Disabled
   Text file          Enabled
   Verbose log        Enabled


0:001> !logo e d
   Debugger           Enabled
   Text file          Enabled
   Verbose log        Enabled
```

© 2012 DumpAnalysis.org + TraceAnalysis.org

Tracing Example

```
0:001> g
ModLoad: 00000000`56bd0000 00000000`56c35000   C:\Program Files\Debugging Tools for Windows (x64)\winext\logexts.dll
[...]
Thrd 1498 000000013F5F1163 ActivateActCtx( 0x000000000044DD58) -> TRUE ( 0x000000000031F8F8)
Thrd 1498 000000013F5F11CD ActivateActCtx( 0x0000000000460188) -> TRUE ( 0x000000000031F908)
Thrd 1498 000000013F5F1201 ActivateActCtx( 0x000000000044E038) -> TRUE ( 0x000000000031F8F0)
(13f0.1498): Unknown exception - code 00000001 (first chance)
(13f0.1498): Unknown exception - code c015000f (first chance)
(13f0.1498): Unknown exception - code c015000f (!!! second chance !!!)
ntdll! ?? ::FNODOBFM::`string'+0x13ab0:
00000000`77c4fd5c 488b36          mov     rsi,qword ptr [rsi] ds:00000000`030b04d0=00000000030b0470


0:000> kL
Child-SP          RetAddr           Call Site
00000000`0031f5b0 00000000`77ac42d3 ntdll! ?? ::FNODOBFM::`string'+0x13ab0
00000000`0031f690 00000000`56c0d163 kernel32!DeactivateActCtx+0x23
00000000`0031f6c0 00000000`56bed394 logexts!LogHookCallFunction+0x73
00000000`0031f730 00000000`56c0d0e5 logexts!LogProcessHook+0x514
00000000`0031f870 00000001`3f5f1254 logexts!LogHook+0x45
00000000`0031f8c0 00000001`3f5f13db TestActCtx!wmain+0x224
00000000`0031f930 00000000`77ad652d TestActCtx!__tmainCRTStartup+0x13b
00000000`0031f970 00000000`77c0c521 kernel32!BaseThreadInitThunk+0xd
00000000`0031f9a0 00000000`00000000 ntdll!RtlUserThreadStart+0x1d


0:000> g
Thrd 1498 000000013F5F1254 DeactivateActCtx( 0x00000000 0x13AB3BF900000002) -> TRUE
Thrd 1498 000000013F5F1263 DeactivateActCtx( 0x00000000 0x13AB3BF900000001) -> TRUE
ntdll!NtTerminateProcess+0xa:
00000000`77c315da c3              ret
```

© 2012 DumpAnalysis.org + TraceAnalysis.org

Topics

- Catching data corruption
- Software and hardware breakpoints
- Breakpoint strategy
- Disabling and enabling breakpoints

© 2012 DumpAnalysis.org + TraceAnalysis.org

Data Corruption

```
// Worker thread periodically writes a command to a controller
// The controller is implemented as an address in memory
// Corruption of controller memory value is modelled as an exception

DWORD WINAPI WorkItemNormal(LPVOID lpParameter)
{
    Controller = COMMAND;

    while(1)
    {
        Sleep(WAIT);
        if (Controller != COMMAND)
        {
            RaiseException(0xBADC, 0, 1, (const ULONG_PTR *)&Controller);
        }
        Controller = COMMAND; // we remember the address of this instruction
    }
}
```

© 2012 DumpAnalysis.org + TraceAnalysis.org

Breakpoint Strategy

```c
// Enable hardware write access breakpoint

DWORD WINAPI WorkItemNormal(LPVOID lpParameter)
{
    Controller = COMMAND; // expect a breakpoint hit here, ignore

    while(1)
    {
        Sleep(WAIT);
        if (Controller != COMMAND)
        {
            RaiseException(0xBADC, 0, 1, (const ULONG_PTR *)&Controller);
        }
        // Disable hardware write access breakpoint, ignore
        Controller = COMMAND;
        // Enable hardware write access breakpoint, resume
    }
}
```

© 2012 DumpAnalysis.org + TraceAnalysis.org

Debugger Output

```
0:001> ba w4 Controller

0:001> bp MixedBreakpoints!WorkItemNormal+0x4a "bd 0; t"  * disable, skip

0:001> u MixedBreakpoints!WorkItemNormal+0x4a
MixedBreakpoints!WorkItemNormal+0x4a:
00000001`3fe414ea c705ecaa000010000000 mov dword ptr [MixedBreakpoints!Controller (00000001`3fe4bfe0)],10h
00000001`3fe414f4 ebbd [...]

0:001> bp 00000001`3fe414f4 "be 0; g"  * enable, resume

0:001> bl
 0 e 00000001`3f03bfe0 w 4 0001 (0001)  0:**** MixedBreakpoints!Controller
 1 e 00000001`3f0314ea 0001 (0001)  0:**** MixedBreakpoints!WorkItemNormal+0x4a "bd 0; t"
 2 e 00000001`3f0314f4 0001 (0001)  0:**** MixedBreakpoints!WorkItemNormal+0x54 "be 0; g"

0:001> g; g   * we skip the first write
Breakpoint 0 hit
Breakpoint 0 hit
MixedBreakpoints!WorkItemDefect+0x12:
00000001`3fdc1512 33c0            xor     eax,eax

0:002> k
Child-SP          RetAddr           Call Site
00000000`02f8fda8
00000000`02f8fdb0 00000000`76d5c521 kernel32!BaseThreadInitThunk+0xd
00000000`02f8fde0 00000000`00000000 ntdll!RtlUserThreadStart+0x1d
```

© 2012 DumpAnalysis.org + TraceAnalysis.org

Commands

ba – set hardware access breakpoint

bp – set software code breakpoint

bl – list breakpoints

bd – disable breakpoint

be – enable breakpoint

t – trace one instruction

© 2012 DumpAnalysis.org + TraceAnalysis.org

Topics

- Platform independent memory dump analysis
- Platform independent MDA patterns
- Exception Thread pattern (on Mac OS X)
- WER vs. MER and WinDbg vs. GDB

© 2012 DumpAnalysis.org + TraceAnalysis.org

Exception Thread

```c
void bar()
{
    int *p = NULL;

    *p = 1;
}

void foo()
{
    bar();
}

int main(int argc, const char * argv[])
{
    foo();
    return 0;
}
```

© 2012 DumpAnalysis.org + TraceAnalysis.org

Xcode

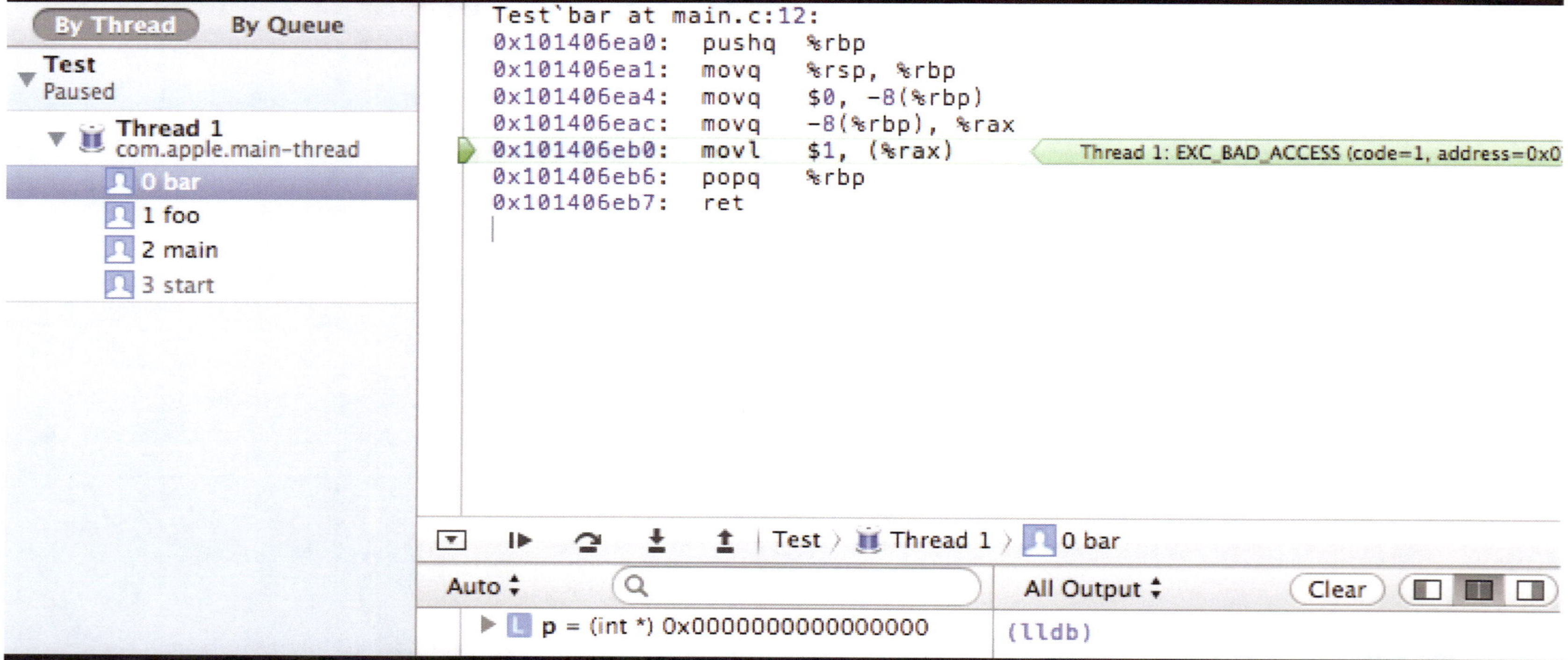

© 2012 DumpAnalysis.org + TraceAnalysis.org

Terminal and GDB

```
Dmitrys-MacBook-Air:/ DumpAnalysis$ ulimit -c unlimited

Dmitrys-MacBook-Air:/ DumpAnalysis$ ulimit -a
core file size            (blocks, -c) unlimited
[…]

Dmitrys-MacBook-Air:/ DumpAnalysis$
/Users/DumpAnalysis/Library/Developer/Xcode/DerivedData/Test-
adsepuwnmyotiyfiajcuyqrwjzmy/Build/Products/Debug/Test
Segmentation fault: 11 (core dumped)

Dmitrys-MacBook-Air:/ DumpAnalysis$ ls /cores
core.5494

Dmitrys-MacBook-Air:/ DumpAnalysis$
/Applications/Xcode.app/Contents/Developer/usr/bin/gdb
/Users/DumpAnalysis/Library/Developer/Xcode/DerivedData/Test-
adsepuwnmyotiyfiajcuyqrwjzmy/Build/Products/Debug/Test /cores/core.5494
```

© 2012 DumpAnalysis.org + TraceAnalysis.org

Debugger Output

```
GNU gdb 6.3.50-20050815 (Apple version gdb-1752) (Sat Jan 28 03:02:46 UTC 2012)
Copyright 2004 Free Software Foundation, Inc.
GDB is free software, covered by the GNU General Public License, and you are
welcome to change it and/or distribute copies of it under certain conditions.
Type "show copying" to see the conditions.
There is absolutely no warranty for GDB.  Type "show warranty" for details.
This GDB was configured as "x86_64-apple-darwin"...
Reading symbols for shared libraries .. done


Reading symbols for shared libraries . done
Reading symbols for shared libraries ......................... done
#0  0x000000010eb07eb0 in bar ()
    at /Users/DumpAnalysis/Documents/MacOSX-Debugging/Test/Test/Test/main.c:15
15              *p = 1;
(gdb) where
#0  0x000000010eb07eb0 in bar ()
    at /Users/DumpAnalysis/Documents/MacOSX-Debugging/Test/Test/Test/main.c:15
#1  0x000000010eb07ec9 in foo ()
    at /Users/DumpAnalysis/Documents/MacOSX-Debugging/Test/Test/Test/main.c:20
#2  0x000000010eb07eeb in main (argc=1,
    argv=0x7fff6e706ad0)
    at /Users/DumpAnalysis/Documents/MacOSX-Debugging/Test/Test/Test/main.c:25
Current language:  auto; currently minimal
(gdb) q
```

© 2012 DumpAnalysis.org + TraceAnalysis.org

Topics

- Xcode build options
- External symbol files
- GDB: Stack trace w/o symbols
- GDB: Loading and applying symbols

© 2012 DumpAnalysis.org + TraceAnalysis.org

Xcode Build Options

Build Settings	Build Phases	Build Rules

Basic All Combined Levels Q-

Setting	■ Test
▶ Architectures	
▶ Build Locations	
▼ Build Options	
Build Variants	normal
Compiler for C/C++/Objective-C	**LLVM GCC 4.2** ↕
▼ **Debug Information Format**	<Multiple values> ↕
Debug	DWARF ↕
Release	**DWARF with dSYM File** ↕
Generate Profiling Code	No ↕
Precompiled Header Uses Files From B...	Yes ↕
Run Static Analyzer	No ↕
Scan All Source Files for Includes	No ↕
Validate Built Product	No ↕
▶ Code Signing	
▶ Deployment	
▶ Kernel Module	
▶ Linking	
▶ Packaging	
▶ Search Paths	
▶ Unit Testing	
▶ Versioning	

© 2012 DumpAnalysis.org + TraceAnalysis.org

Xcode Deployment Options

Alternate Permissions Files	
Combine High Resolution Artwork	No
Deployment Location	No
▶ **Deployment Postprocessing**	**Yes**
Install Group	staff
Install Owner	DumpAnalysis
Install Permissions	u+w,go-w,a+rX
Installation Build Products Location	/tmp/Test.dst
Installation Directory	/usr/local/bin
Mac OS X Deployment Target	Mac OS X 10.7
Pre-install Requirements Property List	
Skip Install	No
▼ **Strip Debug Symbols During Copy**	\<Multiple values\>
Debug	**No**
Release	**Yes**
▼ **Strip Linked Product**	\<Multiple values\>
Debug	No
Release	**Yes**
Strip Style	**All Symbols**
Use Separate Strip	**No**
▶ Kernel Module	

© 2012 DumpAnalysis.org + TraceAnalysis.org

Xcode Code Generation Options

Setting	■ Test
▼ LLVM GCC 4.2 – Code Generation	
Accelerated Objective–C Dispatch	Yes ⬍
Call C++ Default Ctors/Dtors in Objec...	Yes ⬍
Enable SSE3 Extensions	No ⬍
Enable SSE4.1 Extensions	No ⬍
Enable SSE4.2 Extensions	No ⬍
Enable Supplemental SSE3 Instructions	No ⬍
Enforce Strict Aliasing	No ⬍
Feedback–Directed Optimization	Off ⬍
▶ **Generate Debug Symbols**	**Yes** ⬍
Generate Position–Dependent Code	No ⬍
Generate Test Coverage Files	No ⬍
Inline Methods Hidden	Yes ⬍
Instrument Program Flow	No ⬍
Kernel Development Mode	No ⬍
Level of Debug Symbols	Default [default, –gstabs+ –felimina... ⬍
Link–Time Optimization	No ⬍
Make Strings Read–Only	Yes ⬍
No Common Blocks	No ⬍
Objective–C Garbage Collection	Unsupported ⬍
Optimization Level	**None [–O0]** ⬍

© 2012 DumpAnalysis.org + TraceAnalysis.org

GDB Output

```
(gdb) bt
#0  0x000000010d3b0e90 in ?? ()
#1  0x000000010d3b0ea9 in ?? ()
#2  0x000000010d3b0ec4 in ?? ()
#3  0x000000010d3b0e74 in ?? ()


(gdb) maintenance info sections
[...]
Core file:
    `/cores/core.262', file type mach-o-le.
    0x000000010d3b0000->0x000000010d3b1000 at 0x00001000: LC_SEGMENT. ALLOC LOAD
CODE HAS_CONTENTS
[...]


(gdb) add-symbol-file ~/Documents/Work/Test.sym 0x000000010d3b0000
add symbol table from file "/Users/DumpAnalysis/Documents/Work/Test.sym" at
        LC_SEGMENT.__TEXT = 0x10d3b0000
(y or n) y
Reading symbols from /Users/DumpAnalysis/Documents/Work/Test.sym...done.

(gdb) bt
#0  0x000000010d3b0e90 in bar () at main.c:15
#1  0x000000010d3b0ea9 in foo () at main.c:20
#2  0x000000010d3b0ec4 in main (argc=1,
    argv=0x7fff6cfafbf8) at main.c:25
```

© 2012 DumpAnalysis.org + TraceAnalysis.org

Debugging.TV

Frame 0x0C

Presenter: Dmitry Vostokov

MEMORY DUMP ANALYSIS SERVICES

DumpAnalysis.com

Including Crash and Hang Analysis Audit, Training and Seminars

Sponsors

OPENTASK
Iterative and Incremental Publishing

Topics

- Multithreading
- Multiple exceptions
- Diagnostic Console reports
- GDB commands for thread navigation

© 2012 DumpAnalysis.org + TraceAnalysis.org

Multiple Exceptions

```c
void * thread_one (void *arg)
{
    int *p = NULL;
    *p = 1;

    return 0;
}


void * thread_two (void *arg)
{
    int *p = NULL;
    *p = 2;

    return 0;
}

int main(int argc, const char * argv[])
{
    pthread_t threadID_one, threadID_two;

    pthread_create (&threadID_one, NULL, thread_one, NULL);
    pthread_create (&threadID_two, NULL, thread_two, NULL);

    sleep(3);
    return 0;
}
```

© 2012 DumpAnalysis.org + TraceAnalysis.org

Crash Report

Crashed Thread: 2

Exception Type: EXC_BAD_ACCESS (SIGSEGV)
Exception Codes: KERN_INVALID_ADDRESS at 0x0000000000000000

Thread 0:: Dispatch queue: com.apple.main-thread
0   libsystem_kernel.dylib   0x00007fff854e0e42 __semwait_signal + 10
1   libsystem_c.dylib   0x00007fff8ababdea nanosleep + 164
2   libsystem_c.dylib   0x00007fff8ababc2c sleep + 61
3   MultipleThreads   0x000000010f523ec3 main + 99 (main.c:36)
4   MultipleThreads   0x000000010f523df4 start + 52

Thread 1:
0   MultipleThreads   0x000000010f523e1e thread_one + 30 (main.c:16)
1   libsystem_c.dylib   0x00007fff8abf58bf _pthread_start + 335
2   libsystem_c.dylib   0x00007fff8abf8b75 thread_start + 13

Thread 2 Crashed:
0   MultipleThreads   0x000000010f523e4e thread_two + 30 (main.c:24)
1   libsystem_c.dylib   0x00007fff8abf58bf _pthread_start + 335
2   libsystem_c.dylib   0x00007fff8abf8b75 thread_start + 13

Thread 2 crashed with X86 Thread State (64-bit):
  rax: 0x0000000000000000 rbx: 0x0000000000000000 rcx: 0x00007fff854e10c2 rdx: 0x0000000000000000
  rdi: 0x0000000000000000 rsi: 0x0000000000000000 rbp: 0x000000010f780f10 rsp: 0x000000010f780f10
   r8: 0x00007fff754c3fb8   r9: 0x0000000000000001 r10: 0x00007fff8abf8b94 r11: 0x0000000000000202
  r12: 0x0000000000001303 r13: 0x000000010f781000 r14: 0x0000000000000000 r15: 0x000000010f523e30
  rip: 0x000000010f523e4e rfl: 0x0000000000010217 cr2: 0x0000000000000000

© 2012 DumpAnalysis.org + TraceAnalysis.org

GDB Output

```
(gdb) info threads
  3 0x00000001062ffe4e in thread_two (arg=0x0)
    at /MultipleThreads/main.c:24
  2 0x00000001062ffe1e in thread_one (arg=0x0)
    at /MultipleThreads/main.c:16
* 1 0x00007fff854e0e42 in __semwait_signal ()


(gdb) thread 2
[Switching to thread 2 (core thread 1)]
0x00000001062ffe1e in thread_one (arg=0x0)
    at /MultipleThreads/main.c:16
16   *p = 1;


(gdb) disassemble 0x00000001062ffe1e
Dump of assembler code for function thread_one:
0x00000001062ffe00 <thread_one+0>:       push    %rbp
0x00000001062ffe01 <thread_one+1>:       mov     %rsp,%rbp
0x00000001062ffe04 <thread_one+4>:       mov     $0x0,%rax
0x00000001062ffe0e <thread_one+14>:      mov     %rdi,-0x8(%rbp)
0x00000001062ffe12 <thread_one+18>:      movq    $0x0,-0x10(%rbp)
0x00000001062ffe1a <thread_one+26>:      mov     -0x10(%rbp),%rdi
0x00000001062ffe1e <thread_one+30>:      movl    $0x1,(%rdi)
0x00000001062ffe24 <thread_one+36>:      pop     %rbp
0x00000001062ffe25 <thread_one+37>:      retq
End of assembler dump.


(gdb) info registers rdi
rdi            0x0      0
```

© 2012 DumpAnalysis.org + TraceAnalysis.org

Debugging.TV

Frame 0x0D

Presenter: Dmitry Vostokov

MEMORY DUMP ANALYSIS SERVICES

DumpAnalysis.com

Including Crash and Hang Analysis Audit, Training and Seminars

Sponsors

OPENTASK
Iterative and Incremental Publishing

Topics

- Spiking Thread pattern
- Manual core dump generation

✓ *Dump and kill:*

```
kill -s SIGQUIT <PID>
```

✓ *Dump and continue:*

http://osxbook.com/book/bonus/chapter8/core/

- Live thread inspection

© 2012 DumpAnalysis.org + TraceAnalysis.org

Spiking Thread

```c
void * thread_one (void *arg)
{
    while (1) { sleep (1); }

    return 0;
}

void * thread_two (void *arg)
{
    while (1) { sleep (2); }

    return 0;
}

void * thread_three (void *arg)
{
    while (1) { *(double*)arg=sqrt(*(double *)arg); }

    return 0;
}

int main(int argc, const char * argv[])
{
    pthread_t threadID_one, threadID_two, threadID_three;

    double result = 0xffffffff;

    pthread_create (&threadID_one, NULL, thread_one, NULL);
    pthread_create (&threadID_two, NULL, thread_two, NULL);
    pthread_create (&threadID_three, NULL, thread_three, &result);

    pthread_join(threadID_three, NULL);

    return 0;
}
```

© 2012 DumpAnalysis.org + TraceAnalysis.org

Spiking App

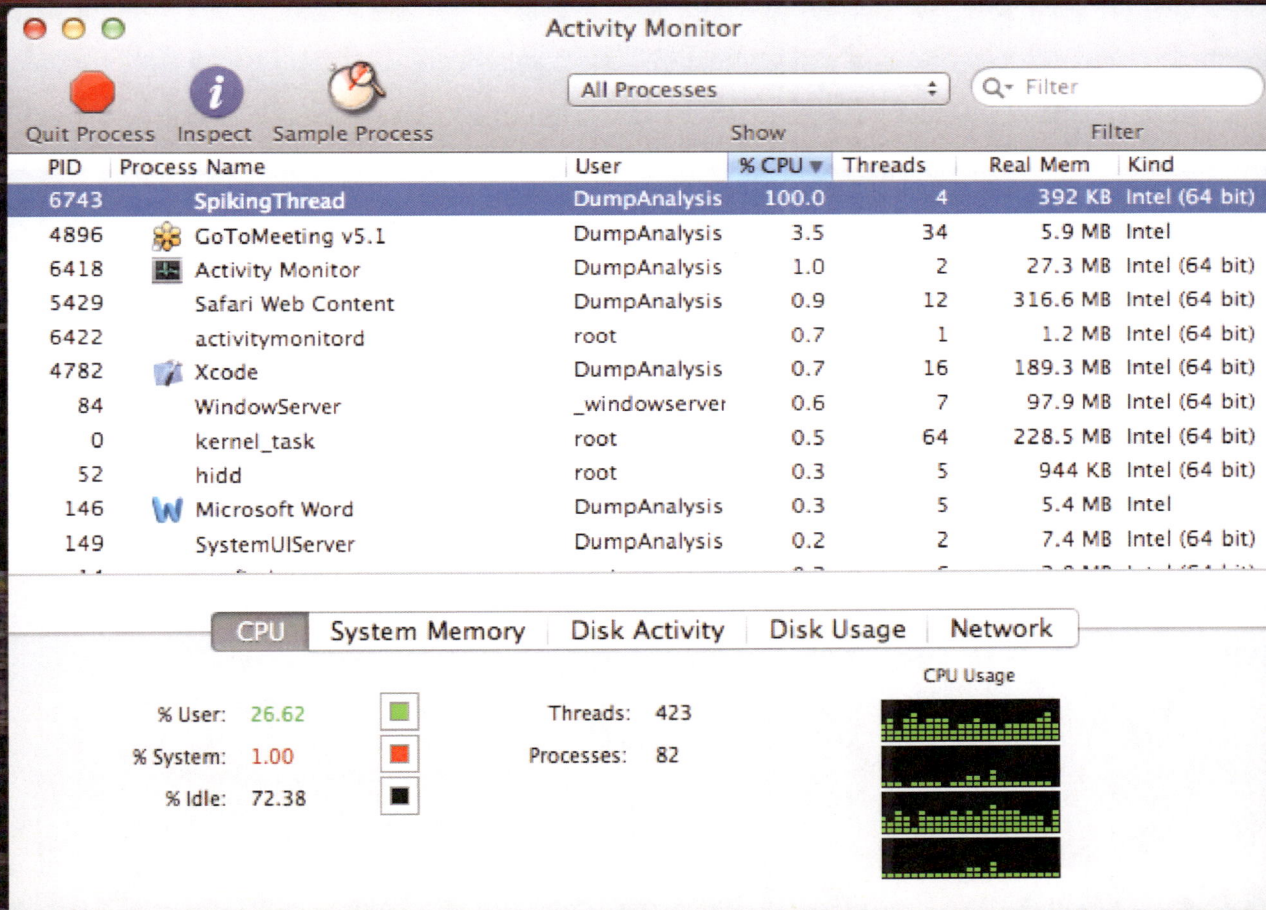

© 2012 DumpAnalysis.org + TraceAnalysis.org

Crash Report

Crashed Thread: 0 Dispatch queue: com.apple.main-thread

Exception Type: EXC_CRASH (SIGQUIT)
Exception Codes: 0x0000000000000000, 0x0000000000000000

Thread 0 Crashed:: Dispatch queue: com.apple.main-thread
0   libsystem_kernel.dylib   0x00007fff8616ee42 __semwait_signal + 10
1   libsystem_c.dylib   0x00007fff8fa7c97e pthread_join + 795
2   SpikingThread   0x0000000107ac1e81 main + 161 (main.c:54)
3   SpikingThread   0x0000000107ac1d64 start + 52

Thread 1:
0   libsystem_kernel.dylib   0x00007fff8616ee42 __semwait_signal + 10
1   libsystem_c.dylib   0x00007fff8fa7cdea nanosleep + 164
2   libsystem_c.dylib   0x00007fff8fa7cc2c sleep + 61
3   SpikingThread   0x0000000107ac1d86 thread_one + 22 (main.c:19)
4   libsystem_c.dylib   0x00007fff8fac68bf _pthread_start + 335
5   libsystem_c.dylib   0x00007fff8fac9b75 thread_start + 13

Thread 2:
0   libsystem_kernel.dylib   0x00007fff8616ee42 __semwait_signal + 10
1   libsystem_c.dylib   0x00007fff8fa7cdea nanosleep + 164
2   libsystem_c.dylib   0x00007fff8fa7cc2c sleep + 61
3   SpikingThread   0x0000000107ac1da6 thread_two + 22 (main.c:29)
4   libsystem_c.dylib   0x00007fff8fac68bf _pthread_start + 335
5   libsystem_c.dylib   0x00007fff8fac9b75 thread_start + 13

Thread 3:
0   libSystem.B.dylib   0x00007fff85b542df sqrt + 15
1   SpikingThread   0x0000000107ac1dc9 thread_three + 25 (main.c:38)
2   libsystem_c.dylib   0x00007fff8fac68bf _pthread_start + 335
3   libsystem_c.dylib   0x00007fff8fac9b75 thread_start + 13

© 2012 DumpAnalysis.org + TraceAnalysis.org

GDB Output (live)

```
(gdb) info threads
  (gdb) info threads
  4                        0x00007fff85b542df in sqrt$fenv_access_off ()
  3                        0x00007fff8616ee42 in __semwait_signal ()
  2                        0x00007fff8616ee42 in __semwait_signal ()
• 1 "com.apple.main-thread" 0x00007fff8616ee42 in __semwait_signal ()

(gdb) info thread 4
Thread 4 has current state "WAITING"
[…]
        total user time: 18446744072923834312
        total system time: 740808000

[…]


(gdb) info thread 3
Thread 3 has current state "WAITING"
        total user time: 816000
        total system time: 3579000
[…]


(gdb) info thread 1
Thread 1 has current state "WAITING"
[…]
        total user time: 635000
        total system time: 5381000

[…]
```

© 2012 DumpAnalysis.org + TraceAnalysis.org

Topics

- Heap on Mac OS X vs. Windows
- Heap Corruption pattern
- Double Free pattern

© 2012 DumpAnalysis.org + TraceAnalysis.org

Heap (allocated)

- Windows

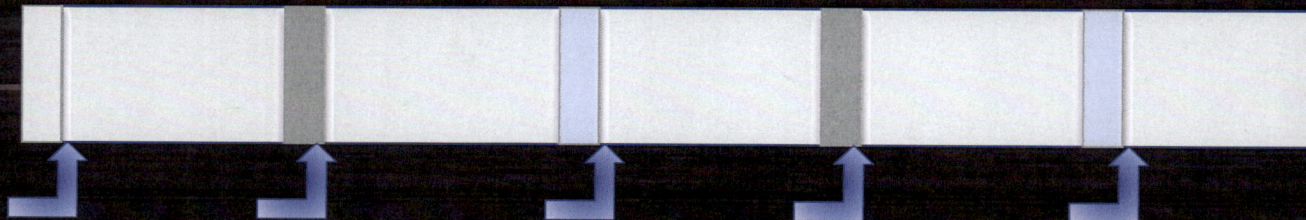

- Mac OS X

© 2012 DumpAnalysis.org + TraceAnalysis.org

Heap (free)

- Windows

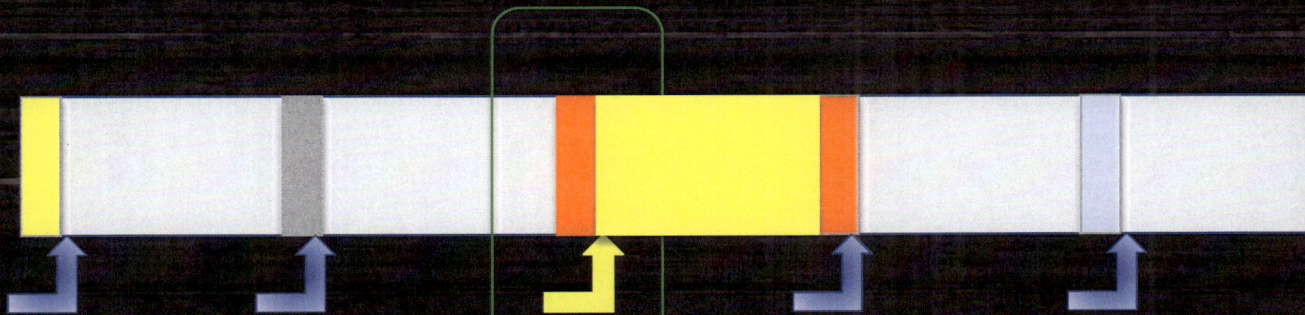

- Mac OS X

© 2012 DumpAnalysis.org + TraceAnalysis.org

Heap Corruption

```
{
    free(p6);
    free(p4);
    free(p2);

    strcpy(p2, "Hello Crash!");
    strcpy(p4, "Hello Crash!");
    strcpy(p6, "Hello Crash!");

    p2 = (char *) malloc (512);
    printf("p2 = %p\n", p2);


    p4 = (char *) malloc (1024);
    printf("p4 = %p\n", p4);


    p6 = (char *) malloc (512);
    printf("p6 = %p\n", p6);


    free (p7);
    free (p6);
    free (p5);
}
```

```
DumpAnalysis$ .../HeapCorruption2/Build/Products/Debug/HeapCorruption2
…
p2 = 0x107000890
p4 = 0x7fd613801400
p6 = 0x107000a90
HeapCorruption2(477) malloc: *** error for object 0x7fd613802408: incorrect checksum for freed object - object was
probably modified after being freed.
…
```

© 2012 DumpAnalysis.org + TraceAnalysis.org

GDB Output

```
(gdb) bt
#0  0x00007fff8479582a in __kill ()
#1  0x00007fff8e0e0a9c in abort ()
#2  0x00007fff8e1024ac in szone_error ()
#3  0x00007fff8e1024e8 in free_list_checksum_botch ()
#4  0x00007fff8e102a7b in small_free_list_remove_ptr ()
#5  0x00007fff8e106bf7 in szone_free_definite_size ()
#6  0x00007fff8e13f789 in free ()
#7  0x0000000106f21e23 in main (argc=1, argv=0x7fff66b20b08)


(gdb) frame 7
#7  0x0000000106f21e23 in main (argc=1, argv=0x7fff66b20b08)
    at …/HeapCorruption2/main.c:56
56              free (p5);


(gdb) x/2i 0x0000000106f21e23
0x106f21e23 <main+771>:     mov    -0x30(%rbp),%rdi
0x106f21e27 <main+775>:     callq  0x106f21e9a <dyld_stub_free>


(gdb) x/s 0x7fd613802408
0x7fd613802408:     "ash!"
```

© 2012 DumpAnalysis.org + TraceAnalysis.org

Debugging.TV

Frame 0x0F

Presenter: Dmitry Vostokov

MEMORY DUMP ANALYSIS SERVICES

DumpAnalysis.com

Including Crash and Hang Analysis Audit, Training and Seminars

Sponsors

OPENTASK
Iterative and Incremental Publishing

Topics

- Raw stack
- Execution Residue pattern
- Effect Component pattern

© 2012 DumpAnalysis.org + TraceAnalysis.org

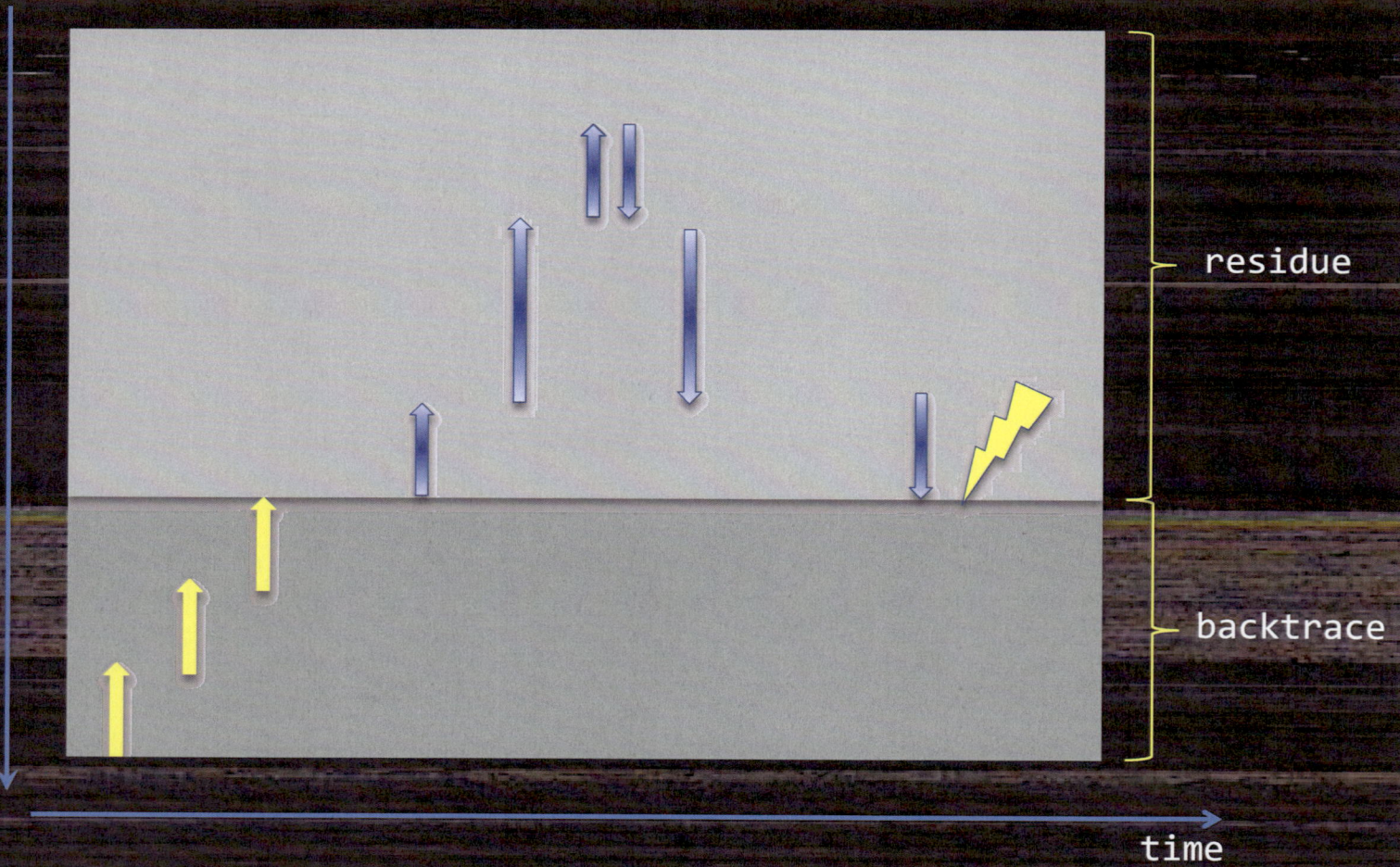

Raw Stack

address

residue

backtrace

time

© 2012 DumpAnalysis.org + TraceAnalysis.org

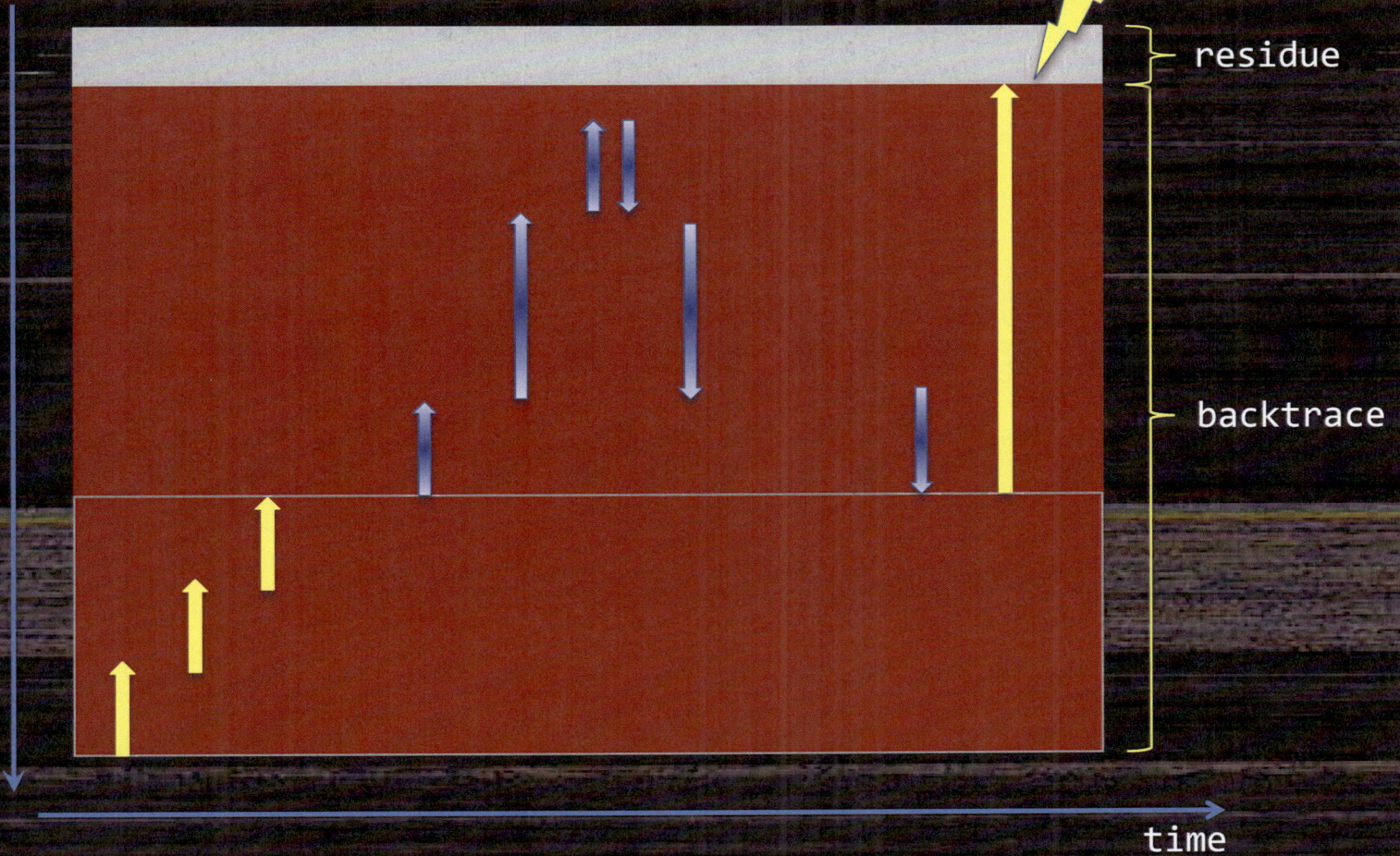

Absent Residue

GDB Output (no residue)

```
(gdb) bt
#0  0x00007fff8616e82a in __kill ()
#1  0x00007fff8fab9a9c in abort ()
#2  0x000000010e3c7c39 in bar_5 ()
#3  0x000000010e3c7c49 in bar_4 ()
#4  0x000000010e3c7c59 in bar_3 ()
#5  0x000000010e3c7c69 in bar_2 ()
#6  0x000000010e3c7c79 in bar_1 ()
#7  0x000000010e3c7c89 in bar ()
#8  0x000000010e3c7cb0 in main (argc=1, argv=0x7fff6dfc6b00)


(gdb) x $rsp
0x7fff6dfc6a38:         0x8fab9a9c


(gdb) x/1000a 0x7fff6dfc6000
[...]
0x7fff6dfc6a30:         0x7fff6dfc6a60          0x7fff8fab9a9c <abort+177>
0x7fff6dfc6a40:         0x0         0x0
0x7fff6dfc6a50:         0x7fffffffffdf          0x0
0x7fff6dfc6a60:         0x7fff6dfc6a70          0x10e3c7c39 <bar_5+9>
0x7fff6dfc6a70:         0x7fff6dfc6a80          0x10e3c7c49 <bar_4+9>
0x7fff6dfc6a80:         0x7fff6dfc6a90          0x10e3c7c59 <bar_3+9>
0x7fff6dfc6a90:         0x7fff6dfc6aa0          0x10e3c7c69 <bar_2+9>
0x7fff6dfc6aa0:         0x7fff6dfc6ab0          0x10e3c7c79 <bar_1+9>
0x7fff6dfc6ab0:         0x7fff6dfc6ac0          0x10e3c7c89 <bar+9>
0x7fff6dfc6ac0:         0x7fff6dfc6ae0          0x10e3c7cb0 <main+32>
0x7fff6dfc6ad0:         0x7fff6dfc6b00          0x1
0x7fff6dfc6ae0:         0x7fff6dfc6af0          0x10e3c7b84 <start+52>
[...]
```

© 2012 DumpAnalysis.org + TraceAnalysis.org

GDB Output (residue)

```
(gdb) x $rsp
0x7fff6b714a38:          0x8fab9a9c


(gdb) x/1000a 0x7fff6b714000
[...]
0x7fff6b714610:          0x100000000              0xbb15000
0x7fff6b714620:          0x7fff6b714630           0x10bb15b59 <foo_8+9>
0x7fff6b714630:          0x7fff6b714640           0x10bb15b69 <foo_7+9>
0x7fff6b714640:          0x7fff6b714650           0x10bb15b79 <foo_6+9>
0x7fff6b714650:          0x7fff6b714660           0x10bb15b89 <foo_5+9>
0x7fff6b714660:          0x7fff6b714670           0x10bb15b99 <foo_4+9>
0x7fff6b714670:          0x7fff6b714680           0x10bb15ba9 <foo_3+9>
0x7fff6b714680:          0x7fff6b714690           0x10bb15bb9 <foo_2+9>
0x7fff6b714690:          0x7fff6b7146a0           0x10bb15bc9 <foo_1+9>
0x7fff6b7146a0:          0x7fff6b714ac0           0x10bb15bee <foo+30>
0x7fff6b7146b0:          0x0            0x0
[...]
0x7fff6b714a50:          0x7fffffffffdf           0x0
0x7fff6b714a60:          0x7fff6b714a70           0x10bb15c29 <bar_5+9>
0x7fff6b714a70:          0x7fff6b714a80           0x10bb15c39 <bar_4+9>
0x7fff6b714a80:          0x7fff6b714a90           0x10bb15c49 <bar_3+9>
0x7fff6b714a90:          0x7fff6b714aa0           0x10bb15c59 <bar_2+9>
0x7fff6b714aa0:          0x7fff6b714ab0           0x10bb15c69 <bar_1+9>
0x7fff6b714ab0:          0x7fff6b714ac0           0x10bb15c79 <bar+9>
0x7fff6b714ac0:          0x7fff6b714ae0           0x10bb15ca0 <main+32>
0x7fff6b714ad0:          0x7fff6b714b00           0x1
0x7fff6b714ae0:          0x7fff6b714af0           0x10bb15b34 <start+52>
0x7fff6b714af0:          0x0            0x1
```

© 2012 DumpAnalysis.org + TraceAnalysis.org

Debugging.TV

Frame 0x10

Presenter: Dmitry Vostokov

MEMORY DUMP ANALYSIS SERVICES

DumpAnalysis.com

Including Crash and Hang Analysis Audit, Training and Seminars

Sponsors

OPENTASK
Iterative and Incremental Publishing

Topics

- Software Diagnostics Institute

- Software Diagnostics Certifications

- Software Diagnostics Maturity

- Pattern-driven Software Diagnostics

© 2012 Software Diagnostics Institute

Software Diagnostics

Definition:

Pattern recognition in post-construction software execution artifacts

Artifacts:

Memory dumps

Software traces and logs

© 2012 Software Diagnostics Institute

Software Diagnostics Institute

Past:

Memory Dump, Software Trace, Debugging, Malware, Victimware, and Intelligence Analysis

Now:

Everything related to Software Diagnostics

© 2012 Software Diagnostics Institute

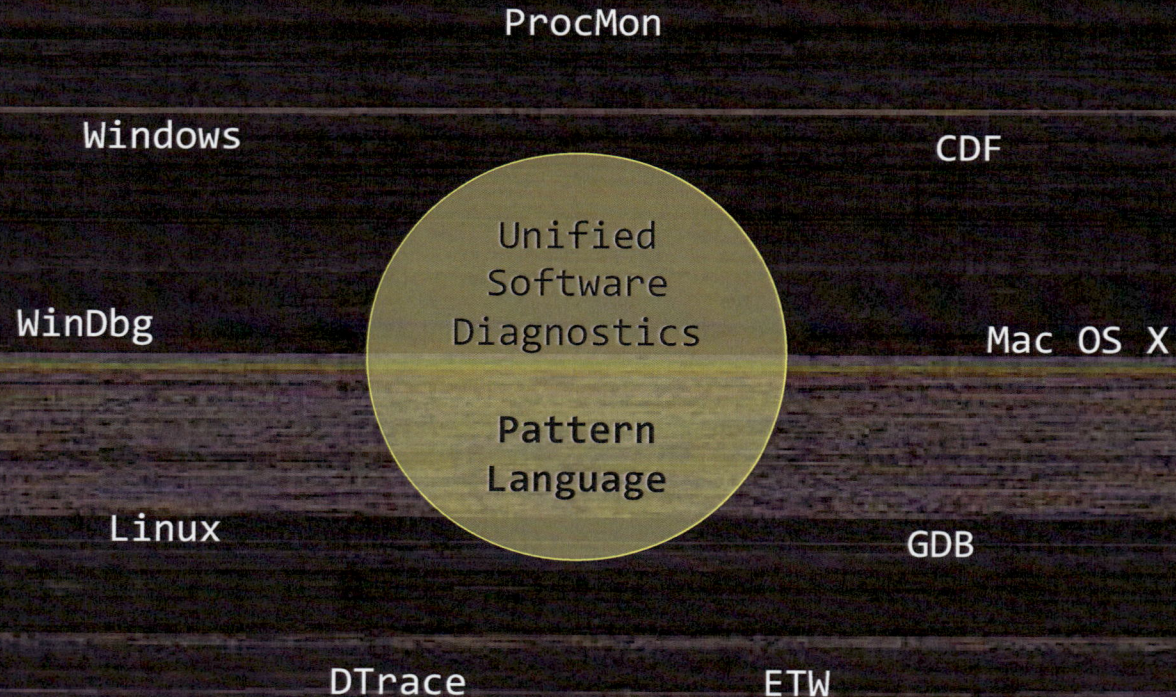

Software Diagnostics Maturity

Past:

Ad hoc methodology and language

Now:

Uniform standards and processes

© 2012 Software Diagnostics Institute

Topics

- Stack region (Windows)
- Stack region (Mac OS X)
- Stack region (Windows, 2nd method)
- Patterns

© 2012 Software Diagnostics Institute

Stack Region (W)

```
0:000> ~
.  0  Id: bdc.8c8 Suspend: 0 Teb: 000007ff`fffdc000 Unfrozen
   1  Id: bdc.aec Suspend: 0 Teb: 000007ff`fffda000 Unfrozen
   2  Id: bdc.674 Suspend: 0 Teb: 000007ff`fffd8000 Unfrozen
   3  Id: bdc.768 Suspend: 0 Teb: 000007ff`fffd6000 Unfrozen
   4  Id: bdc.b34 Suspend: 0 Teb: 000007ff`fffd4000 Unfrozen
   5  Id: bdc.868 Suspend: 0 Teb: 000007ff`fffae000 Unfrozen
   6  Id: bdc.9e4 Suspend: 0 Teb: 000007ff`fffac000 Unfrozen

0:000> !teb 000007ff`fffd6000
TEB at 000007fffffd6000
    ExceptionList:        0000000000000000
    StackBase:           0000000000920000
    StackLimit:          000000000091e000
    SubSystemTib:        0000000000000000
    FiberData:           0000000000001e00
    ArbitraryUserPointer: 0000000000000000
    Self:                000007fffffd6000
    EnvironmentPointer:  0000000000000000
    ClientId:            0000000000000bdc . 0000000000000768
    RpcHandle:           0000000000000000
    Tls Storage:         000007fffffd6058
    PEB Address:         000007fffffde000
    LastErrorValue:      87
    LastStatusValue:     c000000d
    Count Owned Locks:   0
    HardErrorMode:       0

0:000> dps 000000000091e000 0000000000920000
00000000`0091e000  00000000`00000000
00000000`0091e008  00000000`00000000
[...]
```

© 2012 Software Diagnostics Institute

Stack Region (M)

```
(gdb) info threads
   3 0x000000010540ce4e in thread_two (arg=0x0)
   2 0x000000010540ce1e in thread_one (arg=0x0)
 * 1 0x00007fff885e9e42 in __semwait_signal ()
Current language:  auto; currently minimal


(gdb) thread 2
[Switching to thread 2 (core thread 1)]
0x000000010540ce1e in thread_one (arg=0x0)
16              *p = 1;


(gdb) x $rsp
0x1054c0f10:      0x054c0f50


(gdb) thread 1
[Switching to thread 1 (core thread 0)]
0x00007fff885e9e42 in __semwait_signal ()


(gdb) x $rsp
0x7fff6500ba38: 0x8324bdea


(gdb) maintenance info sections
Core file:
    `/cores/core.925', file type mach-o-le.
    0x0000000105441000->0x00000001054c3000 at 0x00037000: LC_SEGMENT. ALLOC LOAD CODE HAS_CONTENTS
    [...]
    0x00007fff6480c000->0x00007fff6500c000 at 0x03a3c000: LC_SEGMENT. ALLOC LOAD CODE HAS_CONTENTS
    [...]
```

© 2012 Software Diagnostics Institute

Stack Region (W2)

```
0:000> ~
.  0  Id: bdc.8c8 Suspend: 0 Teb: 000007ff`fffdc000 Unfrozen
   1  Id: bdc.aec Suspend: 0 Teb: 000007ff`fffda000 Unfrozen
   2  Id: bdc.674 Suspend: 0 Teb: 000007ff`fffd8000 Unfrozen
   3  Id: bdc.768 Suspend: 0 Teb: 000007ff`fffd6000 Unfrozen
   4  Id: bdc.b34 Suspend: 0 Teb: 000007ff`fffd4000 Unfrozen
   5  Id: bdc.868 Suspend: 0 Teb: 000007ff`fffae000 Unfrozen
   6  Id: bdc.9e4 Suspend: 0 Teb: 000007ff`fffac000 Unfrozen


0:000> ~3s
ntdll!NtDelayExecution+0xa:
00000000`7790f9fa c3              ret


0:003> !address rsp
Usage:                 Stack
Allocation Base:       00000000`00820000
Base Address:          00000000`0091e000
End Address:           00000000`00920000
Region Size:           00000000`00002000
Type:                  00020000          MEM_PRIVATE
State:                 00001000          MEM_COMMIT
Protect:               00000004          PAGE_READWRITE
More info:             ~3k


0:000> dps 000000000091e000 0000000000920000
00000000`0091e000  00000000`00000000
00000000`0091e008  00000000`00000000
[...]
```

© 2012 Software Diagnostics Institute

Patterns

Structural memory patterns:

- *Memory Region*
- *Region Boundary*

Unified diagnostics/debugging pattern language (software post-construction):

- **Analysis Patterns**

    Execution Residue

- **Architectural Patterns**

    Command Pipe

- **Design Patterns**

    Memory Region

- **Implementation Patterns**

    Memory address attributes

- **Usage Patterns**

    Memory value inspection

© 2012 Software Diagnostics Institute

Topics

- Software Diagnostics Pattern Language for Mac OS

- Core Dump Analysis Pattern Interaction Example

- Partial Stack Trace Reconstruction

© 2012 Software Diagnostics Institute

Patterns for Mac OS X

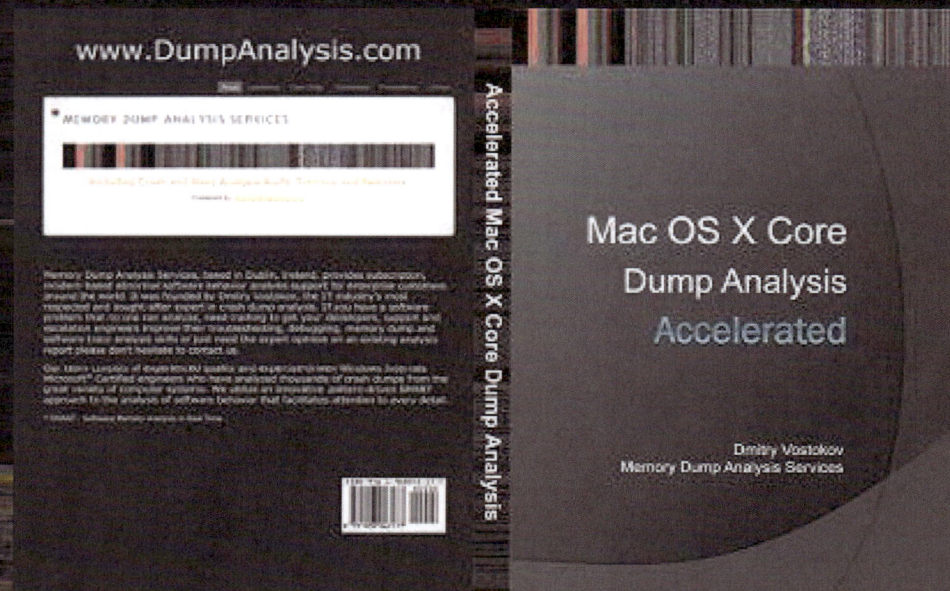

www.DumpAnalysis.com

MEMORY DUMP ANALYSIS SERVICES

Mac OS X Core
Dump Analysis
Accelerated

Dmitry Vostokov
Memory Dump Analysis Services

Accelerated Mac OS X Core Dump Analysis

ISBN: 978-1908043405

© 2012 Software Diagnostics Institute

Truncated Stack Trace

```
DumpAnalysis$ ls -l /cores
total 2357440
-r--------  1 root          admin   301752320  1 Aug 02:35 core.103
-r--------  1 root          admin   301752320  1 Aug 02:45 core.107
-r--------  1 root          admin   301752320  1 Aug 02:23 core.148
-r--------  1 DumpAnalysis  admin           0  1 Aug 02:46 core.413
-r--------  1 root          admin   301752320  1 Aug 02:30 core.78


DumpAnalysis$ sudo gdb -c /cores/core.103


(gdb) bt
#0  0x00045d6c in l2_packet_receive ()
#1  0x8fea1c9c in ?? ()
Previous frame inner to this frame (gdb could not unwind past this frame)
```

© 2012 Software Diagnostics Institute

Execution Residue

```
(gdb) x/1000a $esp-1000
[...]
0xbffffa48: 0x0            0x9a5664c4 <vsnprintf+12>           0x91796 <pcap_read_bpf+17>          0x99
0xbffffa58: 0xbffffa78     0x9a566502 <vsnprintf+74>           0xbffffaf8  0x100
[...]
0xbffffa68: 0xacda7524 <__global_locale>        0x9a81c        0x91796 <pcap_read_bpf+17>          0xbffffc28
0xbffffa78: 0xbffffa98     0x920b1 <pcap_oneshot+35>           0xbffffc58  0xbffffae8
[...]
0xbffffa88: 0x110          0xbffffab4  0xbffffab4  0x300000
0xbffffa98: 0xbffffc08     0x91b1c <pcap_read_bpf+919>         0xbffffc28  0xbffffae8
[...]
0xbffffbf8: 0x0            0x45d2d <l2_packet_receive>         0x8a9800    0x8ba0 <eloop_run+12>
0xbffffc08: 0xbffffc38     0x91feb <pcap_next+58>   0x8a9800   0x1
[...]
0xbffffc28: 0xbffffc58     0xbffffc24  0x8a9800     0x0
0xbffffc38: 0xbffffc88     0x45d52 <l2_packet_receive+37>      0x8a9800    0xbffffc58
[...]
0xbffffc78: 0x37323335     0x30373833  0x76732037  0x45422063
0xbffffc88: 0x8fe9e100     0x8fea1c9c  0x0          0x1a3500
[...]
0xbffffd58: 0x0            0x0         0xff0000     0xffffff
0xbffffd68: 0xbffffdd8     0x43c04 <main+1143> 0x2084a0        0x208200
[...]
0xbffffdc8: 0x0            0x2084a0    0xbffffe28   0x0
0xbffffdd8: 0xbffffdf0     0x2356 <start+54>       0x5          0xbffffdf8
```

© 2012 Software Diagnostics Institute

Regular Buffer

```
0xbffffc38:   0xbffffc88    0x45d52 <l2_packet_receive+37>        0x8a9800      0xbffffc58
0xbffffc48:   0xbffffc58    0x9a4e5ca4 <__commpage_gettimeofday+20>0x0         0xbffffca4
0xbffffc58:   0x50185dbe    0x7a161       0x99          0x99
0xbffffc68:   0x20646970    0x72f240e8    0x300012      0x300012
0xbffffc78:   0x37323335    0x30373833    0x76732037    0x45422063
0xbffffc88:   0x8fe9e100    0x8fea1c9c    0x0           0x1a3500
0xbffffc98:   0xbffffba8    0x91fb1 <pcap_next>         0x5e35c <dyld_stub_pcap_lookupnet+2>   0x364
0xbffffca8:   0x4d00030c    0x7863c       0x33c4de9     0x41d7e900
0xbffffcb8:   0xacdac044 <__is_threaded>0x1464         0x8fea1c9c    0x5e35f <dyld_stub_pcap_next>
0xbffffcc8:   0xbffffba8    0x8fe824c8    0x8fea1c9c    0x5e35f <dyld_stub_pcap_next>
0xbffffcd8:   0x1464        0x786bc       0x91fb1 <pcap_next>         0x8fea27cc
0xbffffce8:   0x8fe9e140    0x1000002     0x8fe8234e    0x11
0xbffffcf8:   0x4           0x13e8        0x71354       0x786bc
0xbffffd08:   0x8fea27cc    0x5e364 <dyld_stub_pcap_open_live>     0x8fe6eefb   0x8ba0 <eloop_run+12>
0xbffffd18:   0xbffffbc8    0x8fe6ef6f    0x8fea1c9c    0x5e364 <dyld_stub_pcap_open_live>
0xbffffd28:   0x8fe9e140    0x9a513557 <malloc_zone_malloc+75>     0x45d2d <l2_packet_receive>         0x8a9800
0xbffffd38:   0xbffffc38    0x8fe7fdbe    0x0           0x5e364 <dyld_stub_pcap_open_live>
0xbffffd48:   0xbffffc08    0x1a0000      0x0           0x0
0xbffffd58:   0x0           0x0           0xff0000      0xffffff
0xbffffd68:   0xbffffdd8    0x43c04 <main+1143>         0x2084a0      0x208200
0xbffffd78:   0x59ec0 <base64_table+12068>             0xbffffdf8    0xbffffe10   0xbffffe28
```

```
(gdb) x/s 0xbffffc78
0xbffffc78:            "532738707 svc BE"
```

© 2012 Software Diagnostics Institute

Debugging.TV

Frame 0x13

Presenter: Dmitry Vostokov

MEMORY DUMP ANALYSIS SERVICES

DumpAnalysis.com

Including Crash and Hang Analysis Audit, Training and Seminars

Sponsors **OPENTASK**
Iterative and Incremental Publishing

Topics

- Trace Analysis Patterns
- Optimized Message Pattern
- Return Value Optimization

© 2012 Software Diagnostics Institute

Trace Output

```
$ ~/Documents/MacOSX-Debugging/RVO/Build/Products/Debug/RVO
A 1: created.
A 1: bar called.
A 2: created.
A 2: bar called.
A 2: destructed.
A 1: destructed.


/* Expected
A 1: created.
A 1: bar called.
A 2: created.
A 3: copied.
A 3: bar called.
A 3: destructed.
A 2: destructed.
A 1: destructed.*/
```

© 2012 Software Diagnostics Institute

Source Code

```cpp
class A
{
public:

    int id;

    A() { id = n++; cout << "A " << id << ": created.\n"; }

    A(const A& rhs)
    {
        id = rhs.id;
        cout << "A " << id << ": copied.\n";
    }

    ~A() { cout << "A " << id << ": destructed.\n"; }

    void bar() { cout << "A " << id << ": bar called.\n"; }

    static int n;
};

int A::n = 1;

A foo()
{
    return A();
}

int main()
{
    A a;                    // A 1: created.

    a.bar();                // A 1: bar called.
    a = foo();              // A 2: created.
    a.bar();                // A 2: bar called.

    return 0;               // A 2: destructed. A 1: destructed.
}
```

© 2012 Software Diagnostics Institute

Assembly Extract

```asm
            leaq        -8(%rbp), %rax
            .loc        1 43 8 prologue_end     ## /Users/DumpAnalysis/Documents/MacOSX-Debugging/RVO/RVO/main.cpp:43:8
Ltmp32:
            movq        %rax, %rdi
            movq        %rax, -40(%rbp)         ## 8-byte Spill
            callq       __ZN1AC1Ev
            .loc        1 44 5                  ## /Users/DumpAnalysis/Documents/MacOSX-Debugging/RVO/RVO/main.cpp:44:5
Ltmp19:
            movq        -40(%rbp), %rdi         ## 8-byte Reload
            callq       __ZN1A3barEv
Ltmp20:
            jmp         LBB3_1
LBB3_1:
Ltmp33:
            ##DEBUG_VALUE: a2 <- [%rbp+$-24]+$0
            .loc        1 46 12                 ## /Users/DumpAnalysis/Documents/MacOSX-Debugging/RVO/RVO/main.cpp:46:12
Ltmp21:
            leaq        -24(%rbp), %rdi
            callq       __Z3foov
Ltmp22:
            jmp         LBB3_2
LBB3_2:
            .loc        1 48 5                  ## /Users/DumpAnalysis/Documents/MacOSX-Debugging/RVO/RVO/main.cpp:48:5
Ltmp24:
            leaq        -24(%rbp), %rdi
            callq       __ZN1A3barEv
Ltmp25:
            jmp         LBB3_3
LBB3_3:
            leaq        -24(%rbp), %rdi
            .loc        1 50 5                  ## /Users/DumpAnalysis/Documents/MacOSX-Debugging/RVO/RVO/main.cpp:50:5
            movl        $0, -4(%rbp)
            movl        $1, -28(%rbp)
            .loc        1 51 1                  ## /Users/DumpAnalysis/Documents/MacOSX-Debugging/RVO/RVO/main.cpp:51:1
            callq       __ZN1AD1Ev
            leaq        -8(%rbp), %rdi
            callq       __ZN1AD1Ev
```

© 2012 Software Diagnostics Institute

RVO Internals

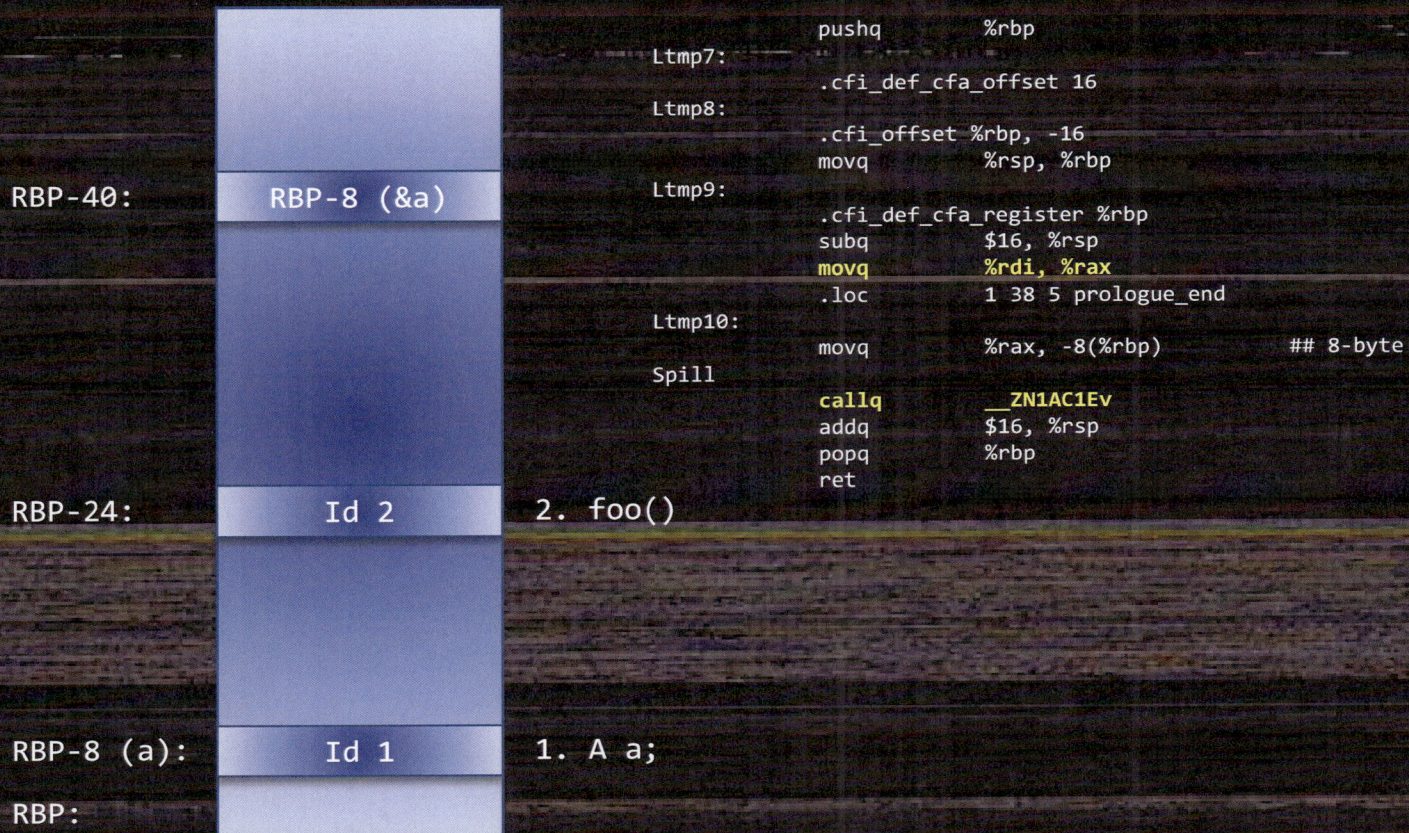

```
                                        pushq        %rbp
                            Ltmp7:
                                        .cfi_def_cfa_offset 16
                            Ltmp8:
                                        .cfi_offset %rbp, -16
                                        movq         %rsp, %rbp
                            Ltmp9:
                                        .cfi_def_cfa_register %rbp
                                        subq         $16, %rsp
                                        movq         %rdi, %rax
                                        .loc         1 38 5 prologue_end
                            Ltmp10:
                                        movq         %rax, -8(%rbp)        ## 8-byte
                            Spill
                                        callq        __ZN1AC1Ev
                                        addq         $16, %rsp
                                        popq         %rbp
                                        ret
```

RBP-40:   RBP-8 (&a)

RBP-24:   Id 2   2. foo()

RBP-8 (a):   Id 1   1. A a;

RBP:

© 2012 Software Diagnostics Institute

Topics

- Thread
- Adjoint Thread
- Software Trace Analysis Patterns
- Examples (Procmon, CDFAnalyzer, Excel)

© 2012 Software Diagnostics Institute

Thread

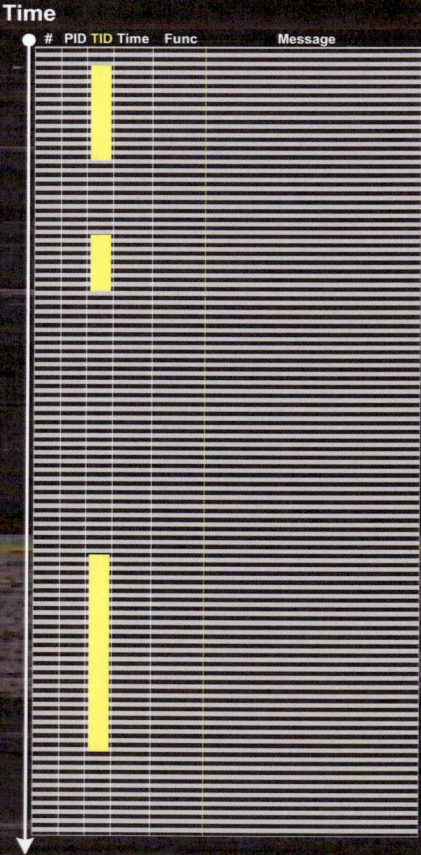

{ msg | TID = N }

SELECT * FROM Messages WHERE Messages.TID = N

<T|A>   <Constant|Variable>

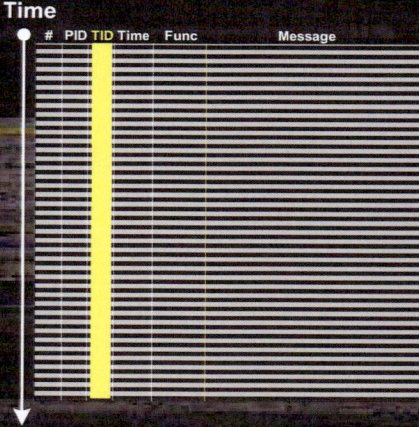

© 2012 Software Diagnostics Institute

Adjoint Thread

{ msg | Func = 'Text' }

SELECT * FROM Messages
    WHERE Messages.Func = 'CreateProcess'

<T|A> <-> <A|T>

From mathematics: Adjoint

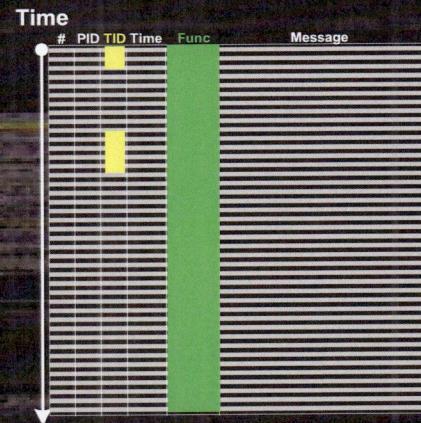

© 2012 Software Diagnostics Institute

Log Analysis Patterns

- **Discontinuity**
- **Time Delta**
- **Anchor Messages**
- **Fiber Bundle**

Complex adjoint
threads:
nested filtering

© 2012 Software Diagnostics Institute

Suggested Reading

Articles on adjoint threading:

- **Extending Multithreading to Multibraiding**

- **What is an Adjoint Thread?**

Tools supporting adjoint threading:

- **Process Monitor**

© 2012 Software Diagnostics Institute

Topics

- Window Message Tracing
- Citrix MessageHistory
- Inter-Correlation Trace Analysis
- Using Excel for Trace Analysis

© 2012 Software Diagnostics Institute

MessageHistory

http://support.citrix.com/article/CTX111068

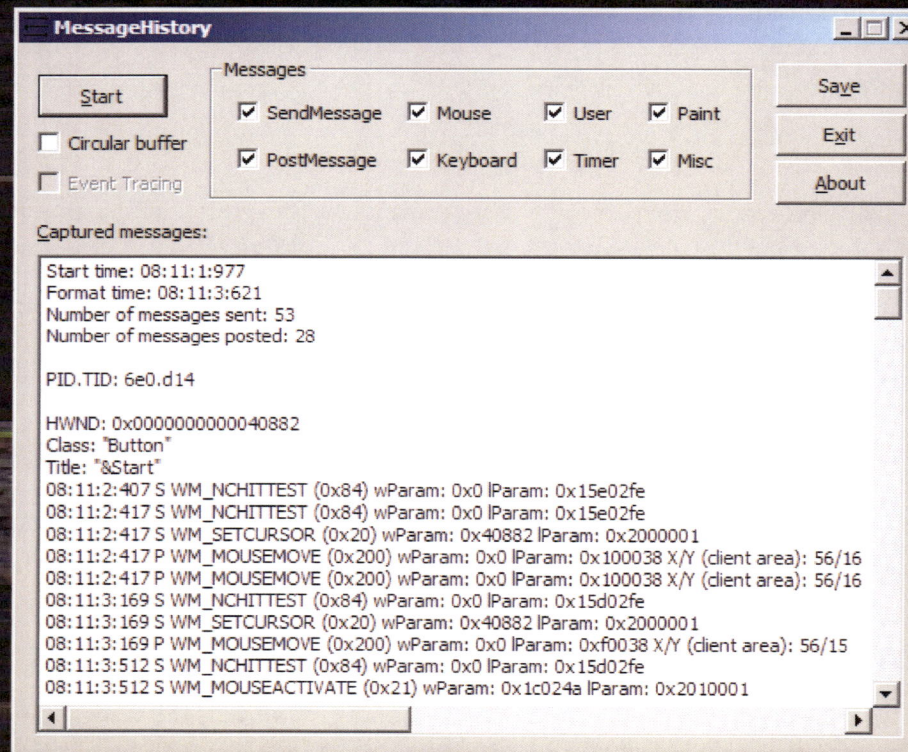

© 2012 Software Diagnostics Institute

Inter-Correlation

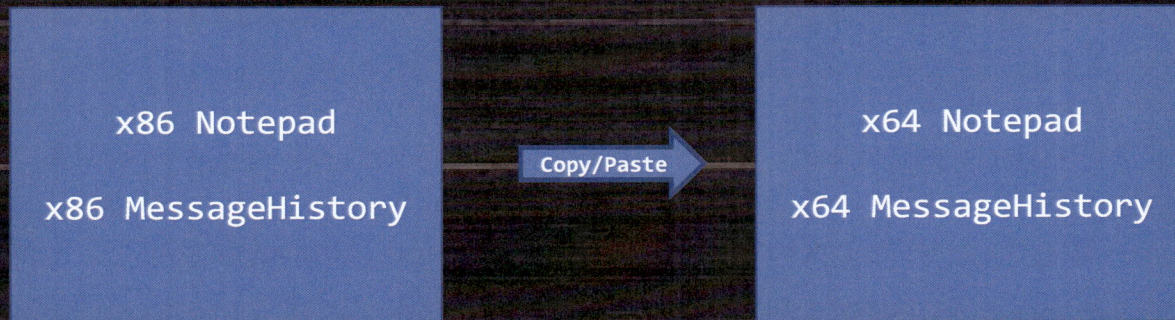

x86 Notepad

x86 MessageHistory

Copy/Paste →

x64 Notepad

x64 MessageHistory

```
148920 08:37:09:420 P PID: d20  TID: 2ac  HWND: 0x002B06C2          Class: Edit Msg: WM_COPY  (0x301)
133333 08:37:13:660 P PID: 128c TID: 11a8 HWND: 0x000000000002D06F4 Class: Edit Msg: WM_PASTE (0x302)
```

© 2012 Software Diagnostics Institute

Analysis Challenges

- Different data field formats

- Different column ordering

Solution: A Proposal for CSTF

Common Software Trace Format

© 2012 Software Diagnostics Institute

References

Trace correlation analysis patterns:

- Intra-Correlation

- Inter-Correlation

Tools for tracing windows and window messages:

- WindowHistory x64

- MessageHistory

© 2012 Software Diagnostics Institute

Debugging.TV

Frame 0x16

Presenter: Dmitry Vostokov

MEMORY DUMP ANALYSIS SERVICES

DumpAnalysis.com

Including Crash and Hang Analysis Audit, Training and Seminars

Sponsors **OPENTASK**
Iterative and Incremental Publishing

Topics

- Window 8 Memory Dumps
- New WinDbg
- New Patterns
- New Commands

© 2012 Software Diagnostics Institute

WinDbg and W8 Dumps

	6.12.0002.633	6.2.9200.16384
Process user memory dumps	+	+
Complete memory dumps	-	+

WinDbg.org

© 2012 Software Diagnostics Institute

Complete Memory Dumps

Stack Trace Collection

```
!process 0 1f
!process 0 16 (with 4 arguments per frame)
```

© 2012 Software Diagnostics Institute

New Patterns

Frozen Process

```
0: kd> !process 0 0

[...]

PROCESS fffffa8002cb2940
    SessionId: 2  Cid: 0c80    Peb: 7f6c41dd000  ParentCid: 0288
DeepFreeze
    DirBase: 2ef45000  ObjectTable: fffff8a002f215c0  HandleCount: <Data Not Accessible>
    Image: iexplore.exe

PROCESS fffffa8003816940
    SessionId: 2  Cid: 0d04    Peb: 7f6c3aca000  ParentCid: 0c80
DeepFreeze
    DirBase: 34024000  ObjectTable: fffff8a001749a00  HandleCount: <Data Not Accessible>
    Image: iexplore.exe


PROCESS fffffa8001e0f740
    SessionId: 2  Cid: 0d7c    Peb: 7f65412f000  ParentCid: 0c78
    DirBase: 0e165000  ObjectTable: fffff8a00055ff00  HandleCount: <Data Not Accessible>
    Image: notepad.exe

[...]
```

© 2012 Software Diagnostics Institute

New Commands

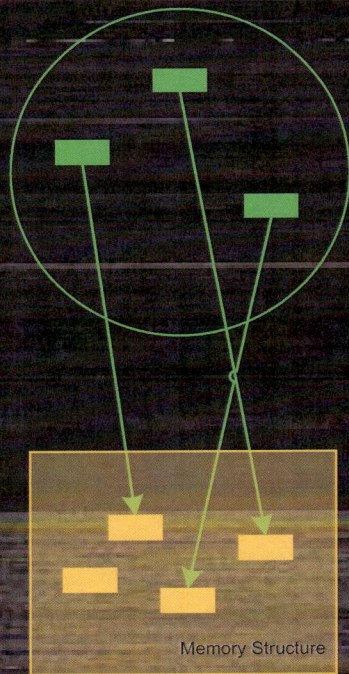

Collective Pointer
structural pattern

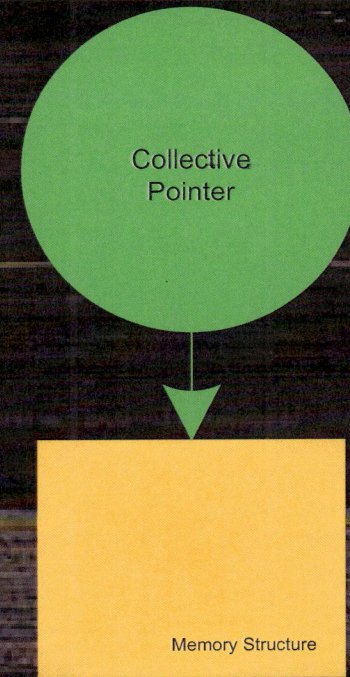

Collective Pointer

Memory Structure

Memory Structure

!for_each_register -c dps @#RegisterValue l1

© 2012 Software Diagnostics Institute

Debugging.TV

Frame 0x17

Presenter: Dmitry Vostokov

MEMORY DUMP ANALYSIS SERVICES

DumpAnalysis.com

Including Crash and Hang Analysis Audit, Training and Seminars

Sponsors

OPENTASK
Iterative and Incremental Publishing

Topics

- Windows Software Log Analysis: A Revolution and Paradigm Shift
- Windows Software Log Analysis: A Comprehensive Training

© 2012 Software Diagnostics Institute

Past and Present

- Searching for an error in a text
- Filtering using an analysis tool
- Looking at a graph

© 2012 Software Diagnostics Institute

A Revolution

- Log as a software narrative
- Structuring analysis according to patterns
- Product and platform independent common language

© 2012 Software Diagnostics Institute

Comprehensive Training

- +100 slides
- +50 patterns in context
- Pattern classification

- Training PDF Preview
- Registration

© 2012 Software Diagnostics Institute

Pattern Classification

- by log vocabulary
- by error distribution
- by log as a whole
- by large scale structure
- by dynamics of various activities
- by message blocks structure
- by log message structure
- by patterns across multiple traces

© 2012 Software Diagnostics Institute

Topics

- Visual Studio 2012
- WinDbg (WinDbg.org)
- Stack Frame Navigation w/o source code
- Stack Frame Navigation with source code

© 2012 Software Diagnostics Institute

Modeling Example

- Modified for crash dump analysis
  GDB for WinDbg Users

- Compiled for x64 under Visual C++ 2012

- LocalDumps on Windows 7

- WinDbg from Windows SDK for Windows 8

© 2012 Software Diagnostics Institute

Source Fragment

```c
int main()
{
        int    local_0 = 0;
        char *hello = "Hello Crash!";

        g_val_1 = 1;
        g_val_2 = '1';

        func_1(g_val_1, g_val_2, (int *)g_pval_1, (char *)g_pval_2);
        return 0;
}

void func_1(int param_1, char param_2, int *param_3, char *param_4)
{
        int local_1 = 1;

        g_val_1 = 2;
        g_val_2 = '2';

        param_3 = &local_1;

        func_2(g_val_1, g_val_2, param_3, param_4);
}
```

© 2012 Software Diagnostics Institute

WinDg Log Fragment

```
0:000> knL
 # Child-SP          RetAddr           Call Site
[...]
0c 00000000`0031fb70 00000001`3f9f11a5 FrameNavigation!func_4+0x1f
0d 00000000`0031fbb0 00000001`3f9f1134 FrameNavigation!func_3+0x55
0e 00000000`0031fbf0 00000001`3f9f10b4 FrameNavigation!func_2+0x64
0f 00000000`0031fc30 00000001`3f9f1049 FrameNavigation!func_1+0x64
10 00000000`0031fc70 00000001`3f9f1453 FrameNavigation!main+0x49
[...]


0:000> .frame 10
10 00000000`0031fc70 00000001`3f9f1453 FrameNavigation!main+0x49

0:000> dpa hello L1
00000000`0031fc98  00000001`3f9f21b8 "Hello Crash!"

0:000> .frame f
0f 00000000`0031fc30 00000001`3f9f1049 FrameNavigation!func_1+0x64

0:000> dc local_1 L1
00000000`0031fc50  00000001                             ....

0:000> dp param_3 L1
00000000`0031fc80  00000000`0031fc50

0:000> dpp param_3 L1
00000000`0031fc80  00000000`0031fc50 00000000`00000001
```

© 2012 Software Diagnostics Institute

Commands

.logopen   !lmi

k   .sympath

kL   .srcpath

kn   dc

.frame   dp

dv /i /V   dpa

.sympath   dp @@c++

uf   dpp

© 2012 Software Diagnostics Institute

Topics

- Software Log Analysis Patterns
- Visualization Tools
- Visualization Examples

© 2013 Software Diagnostics Institute

Log Analysis Patterns

- Based on <u>Software Narratology</u>

- +60 patterns (<u>Reference</u>)

© 2013 Software Diagnostics Institute

Visualization Tools

- GUI: Excel

- Command line: splot / tplot

© 2013 Software Diagnostics Institute

Message Density

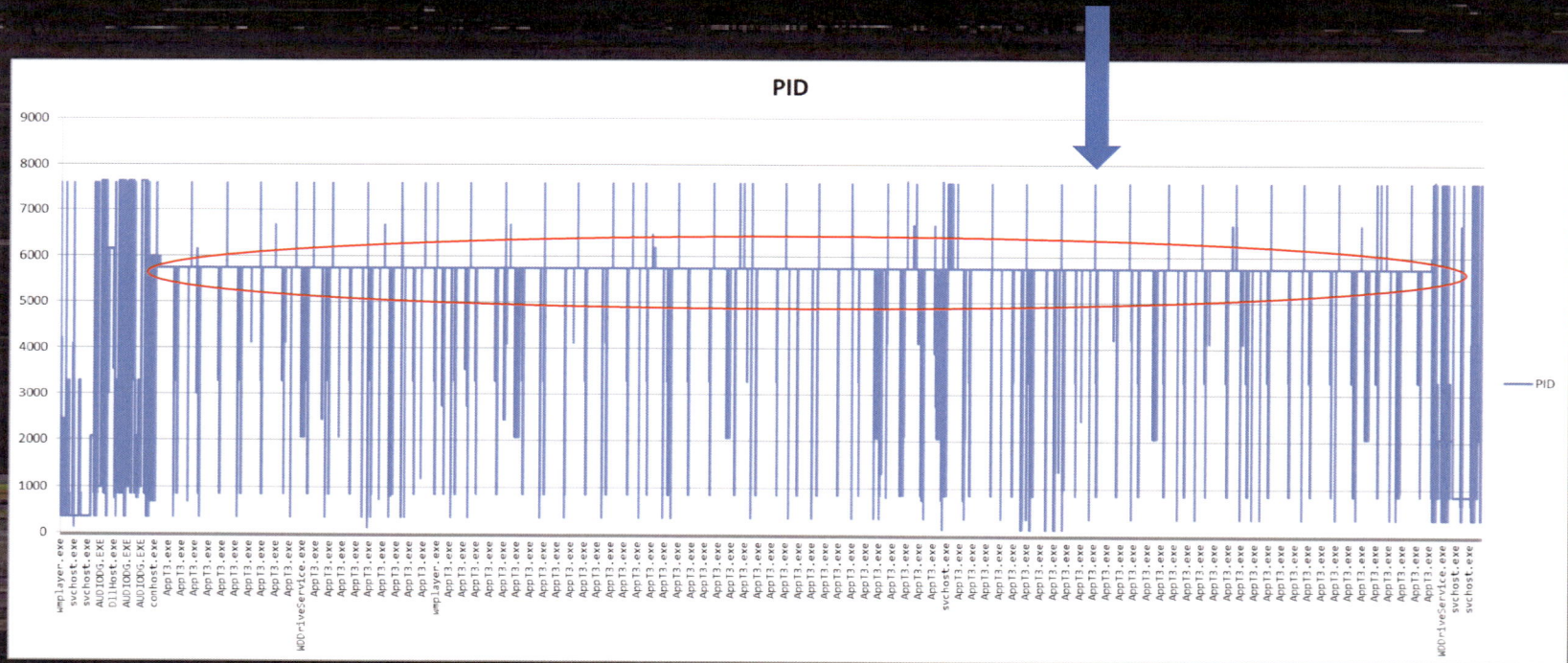

© 2013 Software Diagnostics Institute

Discontinuity

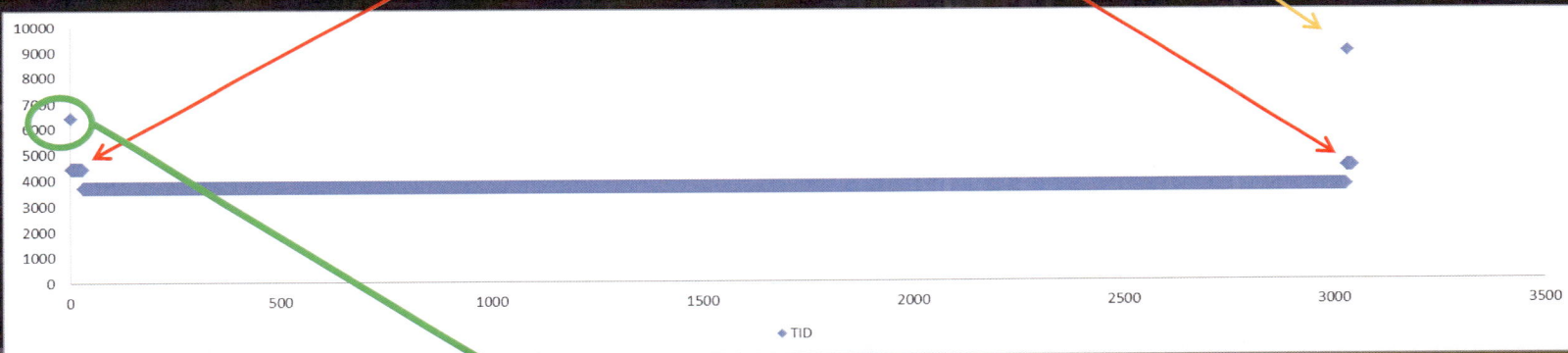

	PID	TID			
23:10:03.0933117	Explorer.EXE 2848	6444	1	Process Create	C:\Work\App.exe
23:10:03.0933232	App.exe 4644	6444	1	Process Start	
23:10:03.0933329	App.exe 4644	6444	1	Thread CreateSUCCESS	Thread ID: 4436

© 2013 Software Diagnostics Institute

Debugging.TV

Frame 0x1A

Presenter: Dmitry Vostokov

SOFTWARE DIAGNOSTICS SERVICES

www.PatternDiagnostics.com

Including Memory Dump and Software Trace Analysis Audit, Seminars,
Certification and Training

Sponsors

OPENTASK
Iterative and Incremental Publishing

Topics

- The Vision of Software Diagnostics

- Patterns of Software Diagnostics Architecture

© 2013 Software Diagnostics Institute

Software Diagnostics

- Software Post-Construction Artefacts

- Pattern-Oriented Artefact Analysis

© 2013 Software Diagnostics Institute

Architectural Patterns I

- Pipes and Filters

© 2013 Software Diagnostics Institute

Architectural Patterns II

- Publisher-Subscriber

Artefact Production		Artefact Collection

Explicit Publisher - active tracing

Implicit Publisher – external memory acquisition

© 2013 Software Diagnostics Institute

Topics

- Memory leaks from social platforms

- Checking for leaks in memory dumps and live

- Searching for evidence

© 2013 Software Diagnostics Institute

Topics

- The life without LSASS

- Fibre bundle memory dumps

- Zero threads on Windows 8.1

- Windows 8.1 File Explorer threads

© 2013 Software Diagnostics Institute

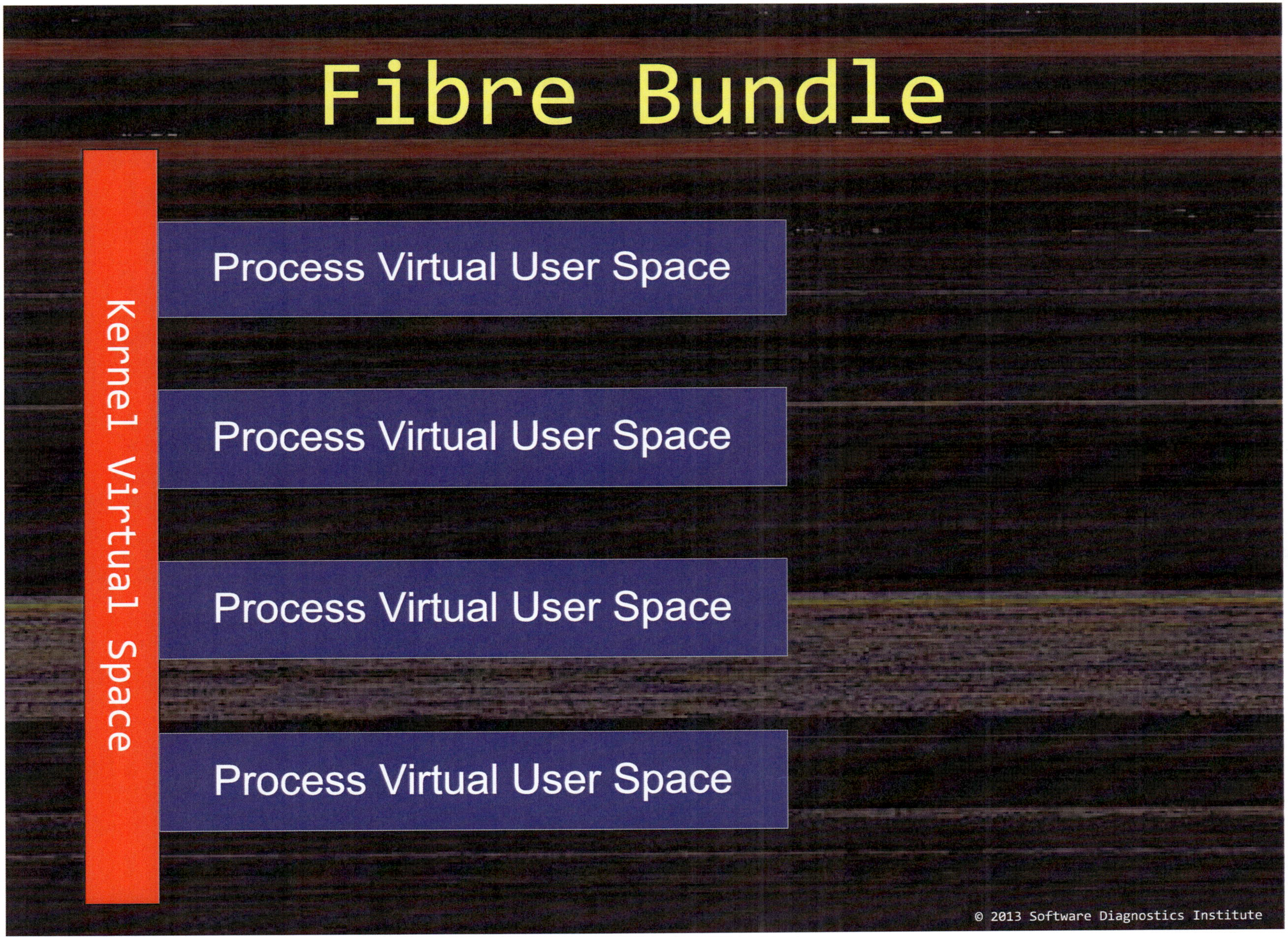
Fibre Bundle
Kernel Virtual Space
Process Virtual User Space
Process Virtual User Space
Process Virtual User Space
Process Virtual User Space
© 2013 Software Diagnostics Institute

Zero Threads

```
THREAD ffffe000006f4880  Cid 0214.063c  Teb: 00007ff70c1a4000 Win32Thread: 0000000000000000 WAIT: (Suspended) KernelMode Non-Alertable
SuspendCount 1
        ffffe000006f4b60  NotificationEvent
    Not impersonating
    DeviceMap              ffffc00001c145c0
    Owning Process         ffffe000021fd900      Image:          explorer.exe
    Attached Process       N/A                Image:        N/A
    Wait Start TickCount   255497             Ticks: 32955 (0:00:08:34.921)
    Context Switch Count   2                  IdealProcessor: 0
    UserTime               00:00:00.000
    KernelTime             00:00:00.000
    Win32 Start Address 0x00007ffe14aed6bc
    Stack Init ffffd00022119dd0 Current ffffd00022119500
    Base ffffd0002211a000 Limit ffffd00022114000 Call 0
    Priority 10 BasePriority 8 UnusualBoost 0 ForegroundBoost 0 IoPriority 2 PagePriority 5
    Child-SP          RetAddr           Call Site
    ffffd000`22119540 fffff802`c572c90e nt!KiSwapContext+0x76
    ffffd000`22119680 fffff802`c572c3a7 nt!KiSwapThread+0x14e
    ffffd000`22119720 fffff802`c56c39a8 nt!KiCommitThreadWait+0x127
    ffffd000`22119780 fffff802`c577ce64 nt!KeWaitForSingleObject+0x248
    ffffd000`22119820 fffff802`c572e289 nt!KiSchedulerApc+0x94
    ffffd000`22119880 fffff802`c57daa23 nt!KiDeliverApc+0x209
    ffffd000`22119900 fffff802`c5ac325c nt!KiApcInterrupt+0xc3 (TrapFrame @ ffffd000`22119900)
    ffffd000`22119a90 fffff802`c57dc3f5 nt!PspUserThreadStartup+0x18
    ffffd000`22119b00 fffff802`c57dc377 nt!KiStartUserThread+0x16
    ffffd000`22119c40 00007ffe`1e2a43b4 nt!KiStartUserThreadReturn (TrapFrame @ ffffd000`22119c40)
    00000000`0d49fcb8 00000000`00000000 0x00007ffe`1e2a43b4


  74  Id: 214.63c Suspend: 1 Teb: 00007ff7`0c1a4000 Unfrozen
 Child-SP          RetAddr           Call Site
 00000000`0d49fcb8 00000000`00000000 ntdll!RtlUserThreadStart
```

© 2013 Software Diagnostics Institute

When CPU Spike is Normal

```
T0:000> !runaway
 User Mode Time
  Thread        Time
  44:1ec        0 days 0:00:20.312
  32:790        0 days 0:00:02.640
[...]


0:000> ~44kc
Call Site
gdi32!NtGdiStretchBlt
gdi32!StretchBlt
GdiPlus!EpScanGdiDci::ProcessBatch_Gdi_Batch
GdiPlus!EpScanGdiDci::EmptyBatch
GdiPlus!EpScanBufferNative<unsigned long>::~EpScanBufferNative<unsigned long>
GdiPlus!DpDriver::FillPath
GdiPlus!DriverGdi::FillPath
GdiPlus!GpGraphics::DrvFillPath
GdiPlus!GpGraphics::RenderFillPath
GdiPlus!GpGraphics::FillPolygon
GdiPlus!GdipFillPolygon
GdiPlus!GdipFillPolygonI
chartv!CvPaintSurface::Polyline
chartv!CvLine::Render
chartv!CvLineChart::Render
chartv!CvWindow::WindowMessages
user32!UserCallWinProcCheckWow
user32!CallWindowProcW
duser!WndBridge::RawWndProc
user32!UserCallWinProcCheckWow
user32!SendMessageWorker
user32!SendMessageW
shell32!COperationStatusTileRateChart::_DrawChart
shell32!COperationStatusTileRateChart::_PaintOverlay
shell32!COperationStatusTileRateChart::_OverlayBufferedPaint
shell32!COperationStatusTileRateChart::_OverlayWindowProcedure
shell32!COperationStatusTileRateChart::s_OverlayWindowProcedure
[...]
```

© 2013 Software Diagnostics Institute

WRL

```
0:000> ~1kc          ; Windows 8.0
Call Site
user32!NtUserWaitAvailableMessageEx
explorer!CTray::_MessageLoop
explorer!CTray::MainThreadProc
SHCore!COplockFileHandle::v_GetHandlerCLSID
kernel32!BaseThreadInitThunk
ntdll!RtlUserThreadStart


0:000> ~2kc          ; Windows 8.1 - coincidental symbolic information
Call Site
user32!NtUserWaitAvailableMessageEx
explorer!CTray::_MessageLoop
explorer!CTray::MainThreadProc
SHCore!Microsoft::WRL::Details::ImplementsHelper<Microsoft::WRL::RuntimeClassFlags
<3>,Microsoft::WRL::Details::InterfaceList<Microsoft::WRL::CloakedIid<IInputStream
Priv>,Microsoft::WRL::Details::InterfaceList<Microsoft::WRL::CloakedIid<CFTMCrossP
rocServer>,Microsoft::WRL::Details::Nil> >,1,0>::CanCastTo
kernel32!BaseThreadInitThunk
ntdll!RtlUserThreadStart
```

© 2013 Software Diagnostics Institute

Topics

- Patterns

  - Heap Corruption

  - Overaged System

  - No Component Symbols

- Checking stack frames for validity

- Global Flags

© 2014 Software Diagnostics Institute

Stack Trace

```
#   5  Id: d9c.12c Suspend: 0 Teb: 7efa6000 Unfrozen
ChildEBP RetAddr
0286f040 770335b7 ntdll!RtlpCoalesceFreeBlocks+0x702
0286f138 770334a2 ntdll!RtlpFreeHeap+0x1f4
0286f158 757714ad ntdll!RtlFreeHeap+0x142
0286f16c 6a9c8413 kernel32!HeapFree+0x14
0286f1cc 6a9587ac mshtml!CAttrArray::Set+0x45a
0286f210 6ae2819e mshtml!CElement::SetClassHelper+0x7a
0286f220 6ad95283 mshtml!BASICPROPPARAMS::SetString+0x15
0286f2a8 6a9c7c71 mshtml!BASICPROPPARAMS::SetStringProperty+0x394
0286f2d0 6acd8401 mshtml!CBase::put_StringHelper+0x4d
0286f2e8 6a8dcac8 mshtml!CBase::put_String+0x26
0286f310 6a8ab793 mshtml!GS_PropEnum+0xb3
0286f3a4 6aa6418b mshtml!CBase::ContextInvokeEx+0x2b6
0286f3cc 6a9b4371 mshtml!CElement::ContextInvokeEx+0x4c
0286f3f8 6a868679 mshtml!CElement::VersionedInvokeEx+0x2a
0286f430 690e6daa mshtml!CBase::PrivateInvokeEx+0x6d
WARNING: Stack unwind information not available. Following frames may be wrong.
0286f494 6915f5c5 jscript9!DllGetClassObject+0x18bb1
0286f508 6915f519 jscript9!DllCanUnloadNow+0x68d08
[...]
0286fa30 6a748904 mshtml!FormsOnTimer+0x55
0286fa7c 767162fa mshtml!GlobalWndProc+0x191
0286faa8 76716d3a user32!InternalCallWinProc+0x23
0286fb20 767177c4 user32!UserCallWinProcCheckWow+0x109
0286fb80 7671788a user32!DispatchMessageWorker+0x3bc
0286fb90 009c362a user32!DispatchMessageW+0xf
0286fbc8 009ee136 sidebar!PresentationHost::Run+0x95
0286fbcc 009f1af5 sidebar!PartInstance::Run+0x8
0286fbfc 7577336a sidebar!StockLib::Utility::t_ObjectThreadProc<PartInstance>+0x59
0286fc08 77039f72 kernel32!BaseThreadInitThunk+0xe
0286fc48 77039f45 ntdll!__RtlUserThreadStart+0x70
0286fc60 00000000 ntdll!_RtlUserThreadStart+0x1b
```

© 2014 Software Diagnostics Institute

Checking Heap

```
0:005> !heap -s -v
LFH Key                    : 0x64ce83ef
Termination on_corruption  : ENABLED
  Heap     Flags   Reserv  Commit  Virt   Free  List   UCR  Virt Lock  Fast
                    (k)     (k)     (k)    (k) length    blocks cont. heap
-------------------------------------------------------------------------------
....List corrupted: (Blink->Flink = 0000003a) != (Block = 066cd2b0)
HEAP 00530000 (Seg 06650000) At 066cd2a8 Error: block list entry corrupted

..ERROR: Block 07b127c0 previous size a0d5 does not match previous block size 4002
HEAP 00530000 (Seg 07510000) At 07b127c0 Error: invalid block Previous

Virtual block: 05f60000 - 05f60000 (size 00000000)
00530000 00000002  32576   28056  32576   2230   296    20    1     2   LFH
...00820000 00001002   3136    1644   1644      7    43     3    0     0   LFH
.01fe0000 00001002    256     144    256      2     3     1    0     0   LFH
..001c0000 00001002   1088     468    468      8     8     2    0     0   LFH
.004c0000 00001003    256      68    256     49    13     1    0   N/A
.02770000 00001003    256       4    256      2     1     1    0   N/A
.00480000 00001003    256       4    256      2     1     1    0   N/A
.024b0000 00001003    256       4    256      2     1     1    0   N/A
.02460000 00001003    256       4    256      2     1     1    0   N/A
.029a0000 00001003    256       4    256      2     1     1    0   N/A
.02950000 00001003    256       4    256      2     1     1    0   N/A
.030a0000 00001002    256     168    256      4     6     1    0     0   LFH
.033c0000 00001002    256      12    256      2     3     1    0     0
..05da0000 00001002   1088     504    504    266    17     2    0     0   LFH
.06b40000 00011002    256       8    256      4     2     1    0     0
.063a0000 00001002     64      16     64      5     2     1    0     0
.06cd0000 00001002    256       4    256      1     2     1    0     0
-------------------------------------------------------------------------------
```

© 2014 Software Diagnostics Institute

Checking Stack Trace

```
#  5  Id: d9c.12c Suspend: 0 Teb: 7efa6000 Unfrozen
ChildEBP RetAddr
0286f040 770335b7 ntdll!RtlpCoalesceFreeBlocks+0x702
0286f138 770334a2 ntdll!RtlpFreeHeap+0x1f4
0286f158 757714ad ntdll!RtlFreeHeap+0x142
0286f16c 6a9c8413 kernel32!HeapFree+0x14
0286f1cc 6a9587ac mshtml!CAttrArray::Set+0x45a
[…]
0286f3f8 6a868679 mshtml!CElement::VersionedInvokeEx+0x2a
0286f430 690e6daa mshtml!CBase::PrivateInvokeEx+0x6d
WARNING: Stack unwind information not available. Following frames may be wrong.
0286f494 6915f5c5 jscript9!DllGetClassObject+0x18bb1
0286f508 6915f519 jscript9!DllCanUnloadNow+0x68d08
[…]
0286fa30 6a748904 mshtml!FormsOnTimer+0x55
0286fa7c 767162fa mshtml!GlobalWndProc+0x191
[…]
0286fbc8 009ee136 sidebar!PresentationHost::Run+0x95
0286fbcc 009f1af5 sidebar!PartInstance::Run+0x8
0286fbfc 7577336a sidebar!StockLib::Utility::t_ObjectThreadProc<PartInstance>+0x59
0286fc08 77039f72 kernel32!BaseThreadInitThunk+0xe
0286fc48 77039f45 ntdll!__RtlUserThreadStart+0x70
0286fc60 00000000 ntdll!_RtlUserThreadStart+0x1b


0:005> ub 690e6daa
jscript9!DllGetClassObject+0x18b9e:
690e6d97 ff7514          push    dword ptr [ebp+14h]
690e6d9a ff7510          push    dword ptr [ebp+10h]
690e6d9d 8b06            mov     eax,dword ptr [esi]
690e6d9f 53              push    ebx
690e6da0 ff75ec          push    dword ptr [ebp-14h]
690e6da3 ff7508          push    dword ptr [ebp+8]
690e6da6 56              push    esi
690e6da7 ff5020          call    dword ptr [eax+20h]
690e6daa
```

© 2014 Software Diagnostics Institute

Enabling Page Heap

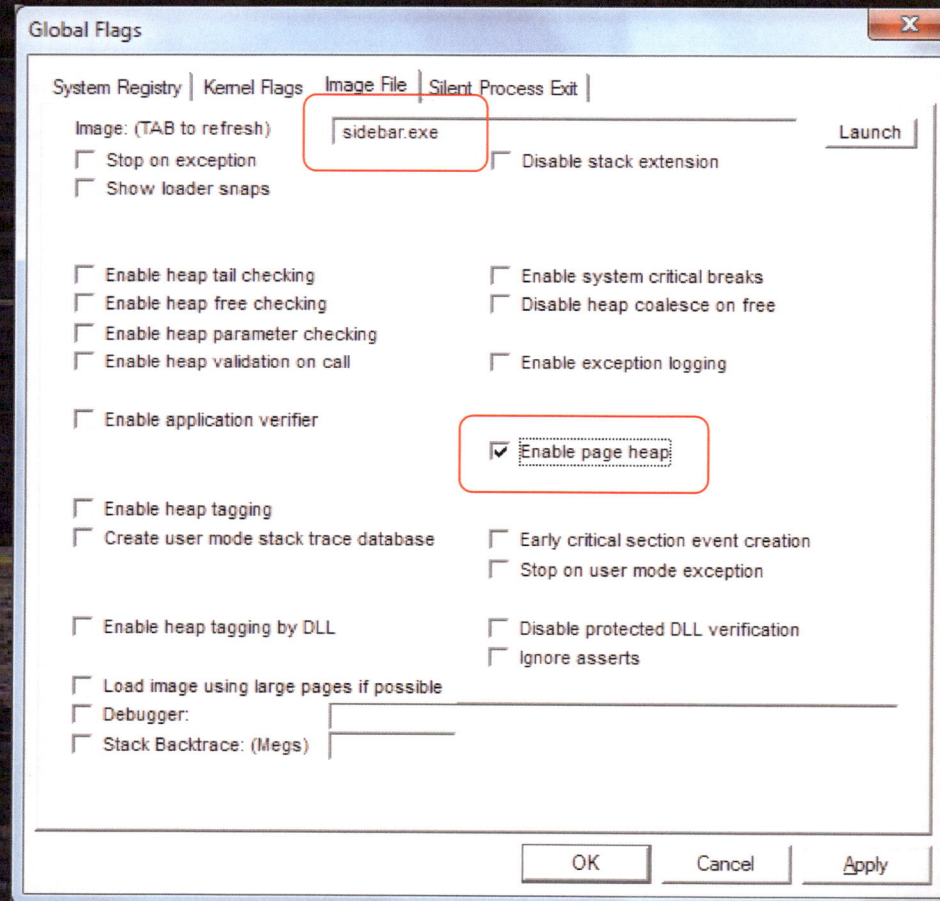

© 2014 Software Diagnostics Institute

Debugging.TV

Frame 0x20

Presenter: Dmitry Vostokov

SOFTWARE DIAGNOSTICS SERVICES

www.DumpAnalysis.com

Sponsors OPENTASK
Iterative and Incremental Publishing

Including Memory Dump and Software Trace Analysis Audit, Seminars,
Certification and Training

Topics

- Malware Analysis Patterns
- Malware Modeling
- Injection Residue
- Example

© 2013 Software Diagnostics Institute

Malware Patterns

Malware:

software that uses planned alteration of structure and behaviour of software to serve malicious purposes.

Malware analysis patterns:

intentional abnormal software structure and behavior patterns

Memory Dump and Trace Analysis Patterns

Malware Analysis Patterns

© 2013 Software Diagnostics Institute

Malware Modeling

Real scenario:

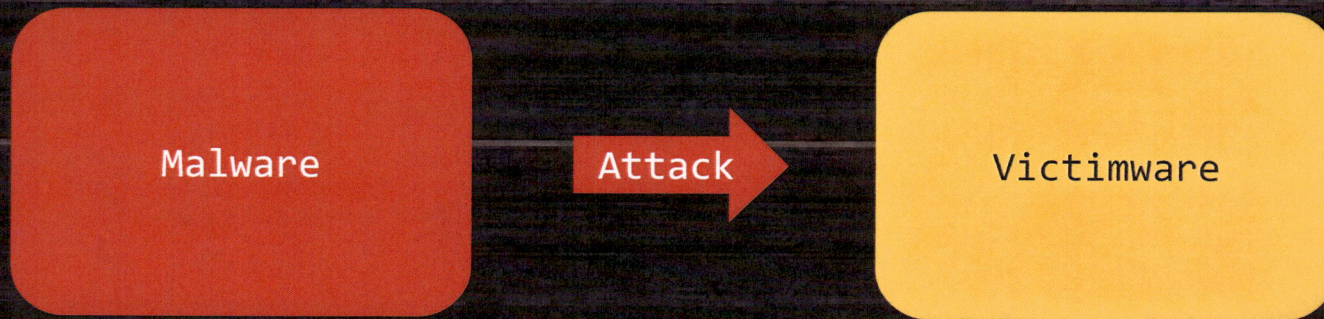

Malware → Attack → Victimware

Simplified modeling scenario:

Coding post-attack effects

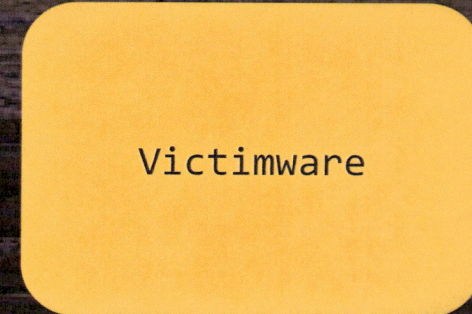

Victimware

© 2013 Software Diagnostics Institute

DLL Injection Example

```
LPWSTR szDLL = L".\\winspool.dll";

int main(int argc, WCHAR* argv[])
{
      for (int i = 0; i < 100; ++i)
            _beginthread(thread, 0, (void *)INFINITE);

      Sleep(10000);

      CreateRemoteThread (GetCurrentProcess(), NULL, 0, reinterpret_cast<LPTHREAD_START_ROUTINE>(LoadLibraryW),
            szDLL,0, NULL);

      Sleep(INFINITE);

      return 0;
}

// winspool.dll

BOOL APIENTRY DllMain( HMODULE hModule, DWORD  ul_reason_for_call, LPVOID lpReserved)
{
      switch (ul_reason_for_call)
      {
            case DLL_PROCESS_ATTACH:
            case DLL_THREAD_ATTACH:

                  StartSpying();  // calls CreateFile(L"RedOctober.dll", …);
                  Sleep(INFINITE);

            case DLL_THREAD_DETACH:
            case DLL_PROCESS_DETACH:
            break;
      }
      return TRUE;
}
```

© 2013 Software Diagnostics Institute

Injection Residue

Execution Residue:

Data Residue

```
00000000`08d4f2c0  00000000`005381f0 ""
00000000`08d4f2c8  000007fe`f6e3e248 ".\RedOctober.dll"
00000000`08d4f2d0  00000000`00000000
```

Call Footprint

```
00000000`08d4f2c0  00000000`005381f0
00000000`08d4f2c8  000007fe`f6e3e248 winspool+0xe248
00000000`08d4f2d0  00000000`00000000
00000000`08d4f2d8  00000000`00000000
00000000`08d4f2e0  00000000`00000000
00000000`08d4f2e8  00000000`76bf18ed kernel32!CreateFileWImplementation+0x7d
00000000`08d4f2f0  00000000`00000000
[...]
00000000`08d4f340  00000000`08d4f3d0
00000000`08d4f348  000007fe`fd4e1203 KERNELBASE!SleepEx+0xab
00000000`08d4f350  00000000`08d4f408
```

© 2013 Software Diagnostics Institute

Topics

- Process dumps: main algorithm
- NTSD and LocalDumps example
- Troubleshooting process dumps

© 2013 Software Diagnostics Institute

Main Algorithm

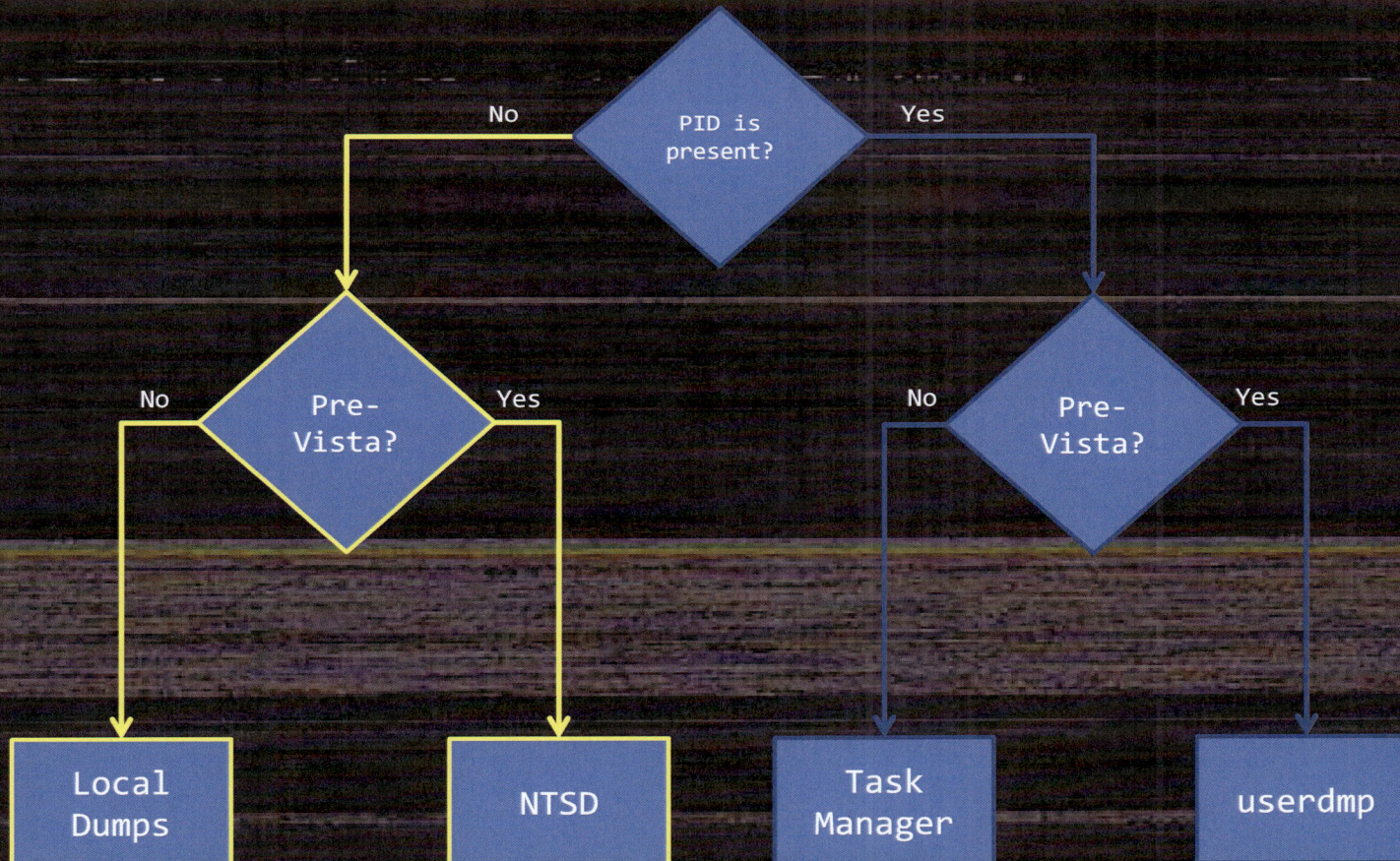

© 2013 Software Diagnostics Institute

NTSD

- x64

  HKLM\S\M\WNT\CV\AeDebug\Debugger =
      ntsd -p %ld -e %ld -c ".dump /f /u c:\NTSDumps**x64**\new.dmp; q"

- x86 on x64

  HKLM\S**Wow6432Node**\M\WNT\CV\AeDebug\Debugger =
      ntsd -p %ld -e %ld -c ".dump /f /u c:\NTSDumps**x86**\new.dmp; q"

- native x86

  HKLM\S\M\WNT\CV\AeDebug\Debugger =
      ntsd -p %ld -e %ld -c ".dump /f /u c:\NTSDumps\new.dmp; q"

- /ma switch instead of /f for new NTSD

© 2013 Software Diagnostics Institute

LocalDumps

HKLM\S\M\W\Windows Error Reporting\LocalDumps

Name: DumpFolder
   Type: REG_SZ
   Value: C:\MemoryDumps

Name: DumpType
   Type: REG_DWORD
   Value: 0x2

© 2013 Software Diagnostics Institute

Topics

- Process dumps: main algorithm
- Task Manager and userdump.exe examples
- Troubleshooting process dumps

© 2013 Software Diagnostics Institute

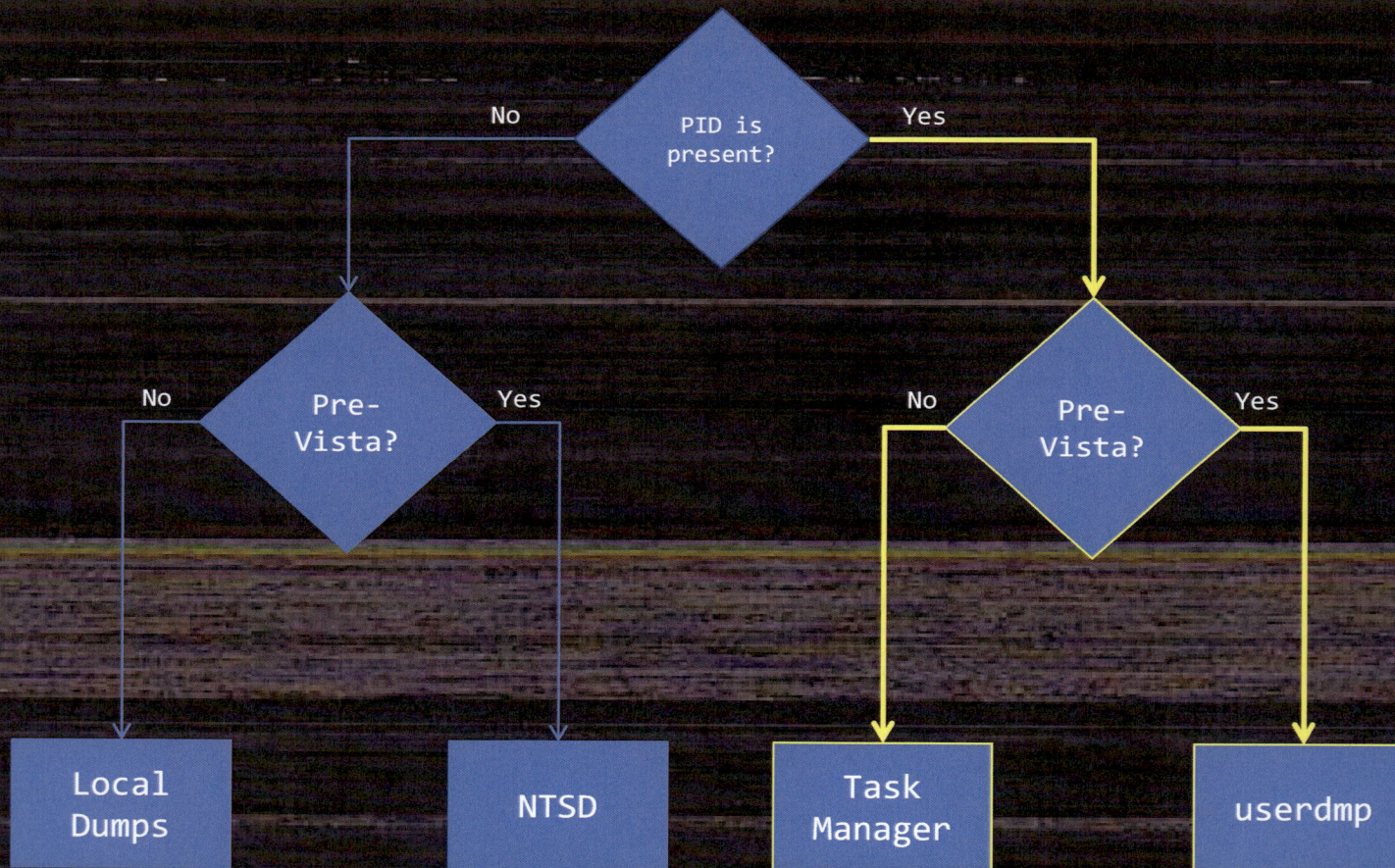

Main Algorithm

© 2013 Software Diagnostics Institute

Userdump.exe

- x64

```
C:\kktools\userdump8.1\x64\userdump -p
C:\kktools\userdump8.1\x64\userdump <process name>|<PID>
```

- (x86 on x64)* or native x86

```
C:\kktools\userdump8.1\x86\userdump -p
C:\kktools\userdump8.1\x86\userdump <process name>|<PID>
```

* May not work on x64 Vista, Windows 7 and higher

© 2013 Software Diagnostics Institute

Task Manager

x86 on x64

C:\Windows\SysWOW64\taskmgr.exe

© 2013 Software Diagnostics Institute

Topics

- Why we need complete memory dumps
- Configuring for complete memory dumps
- Windows 7 and Windows 8 pitfalls

© 2013 Software Diagnostics Institute

Wait Chain

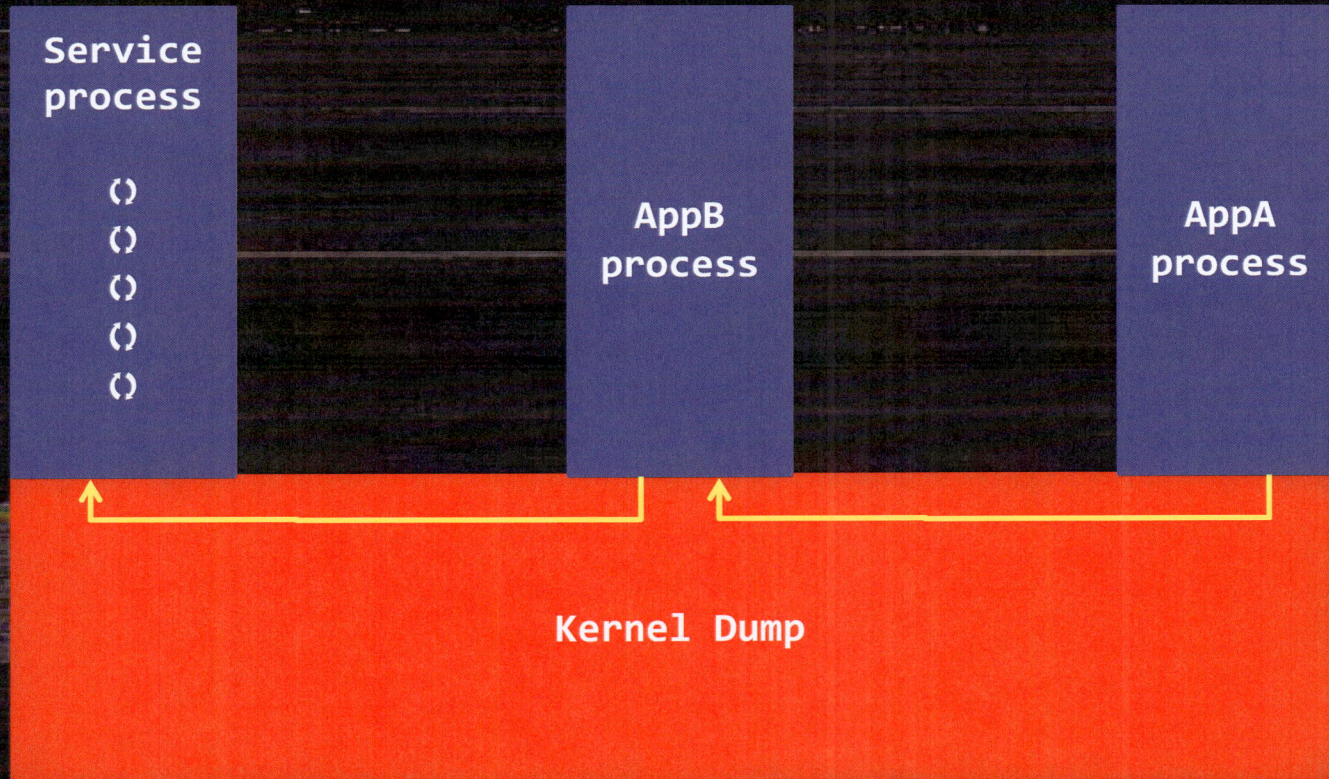

© 2013 Software Diagnostics Institute

0p1

Truncated complete memory dumps

[Truncated Dump](#) analysis pattern

© 2013 Software Diagnostics Institute

0p2

No Complete Memory Dump option

HKLM\S\CCS\Control\CrashControl

CrashDumpEnabled = 1 (DWORD)

© 2013 Software Diagnostics Institute

0p3

No complete memory dumps saved after BSOD

HKLM\S\CCS\Control\CrashControl

AlwaysKeepMemoryDump = 1 (DWORD)

© 2013 Software Diagnostics Institute

Topics

- Raw stack
- Execution Residue pattern
- Manual stack reconstruction
- New! Past Stack Trace pattern

© 2013 Software Diagnostics Institute

Raw Stack

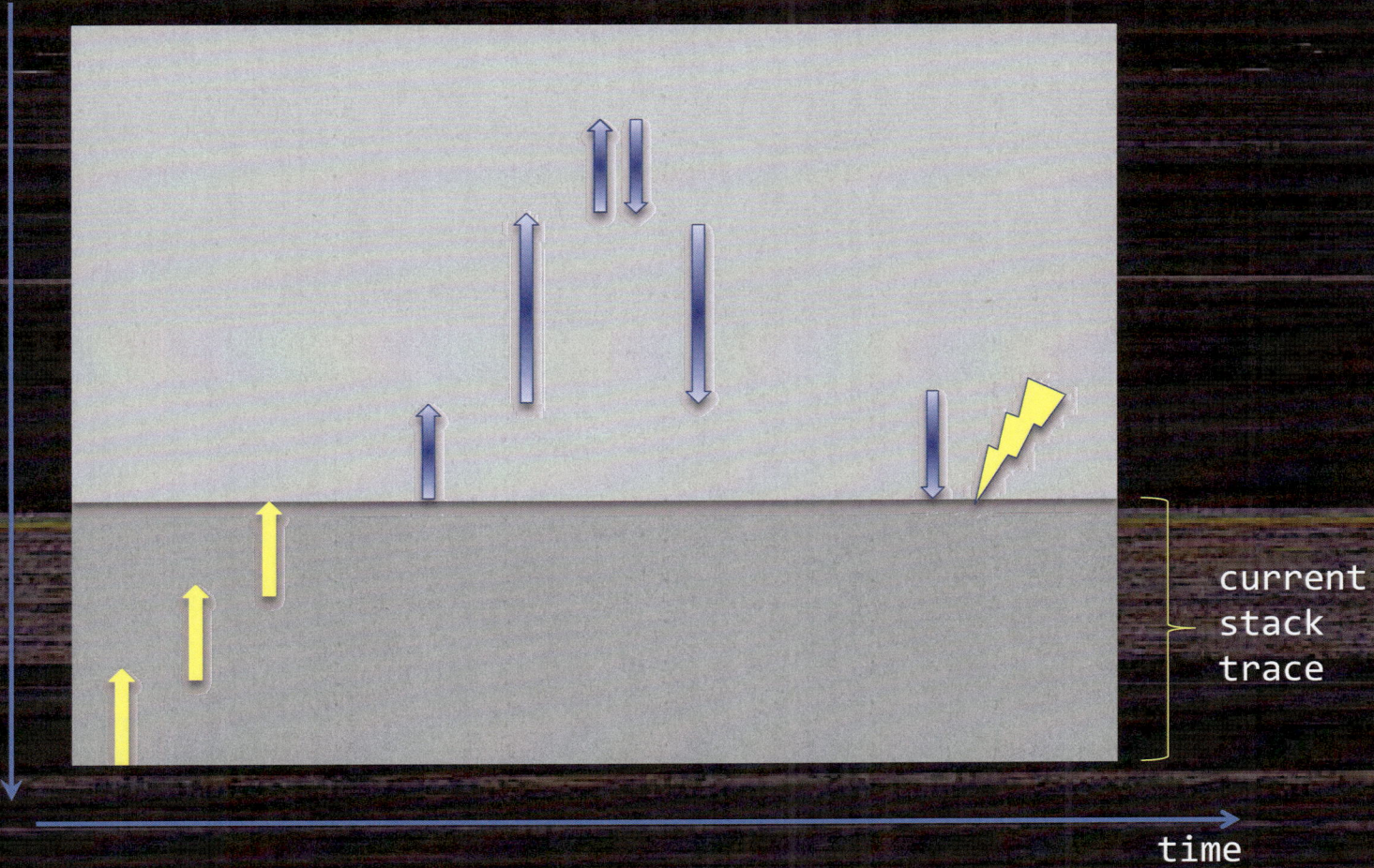

© 2013 Software Diagnostics Institute

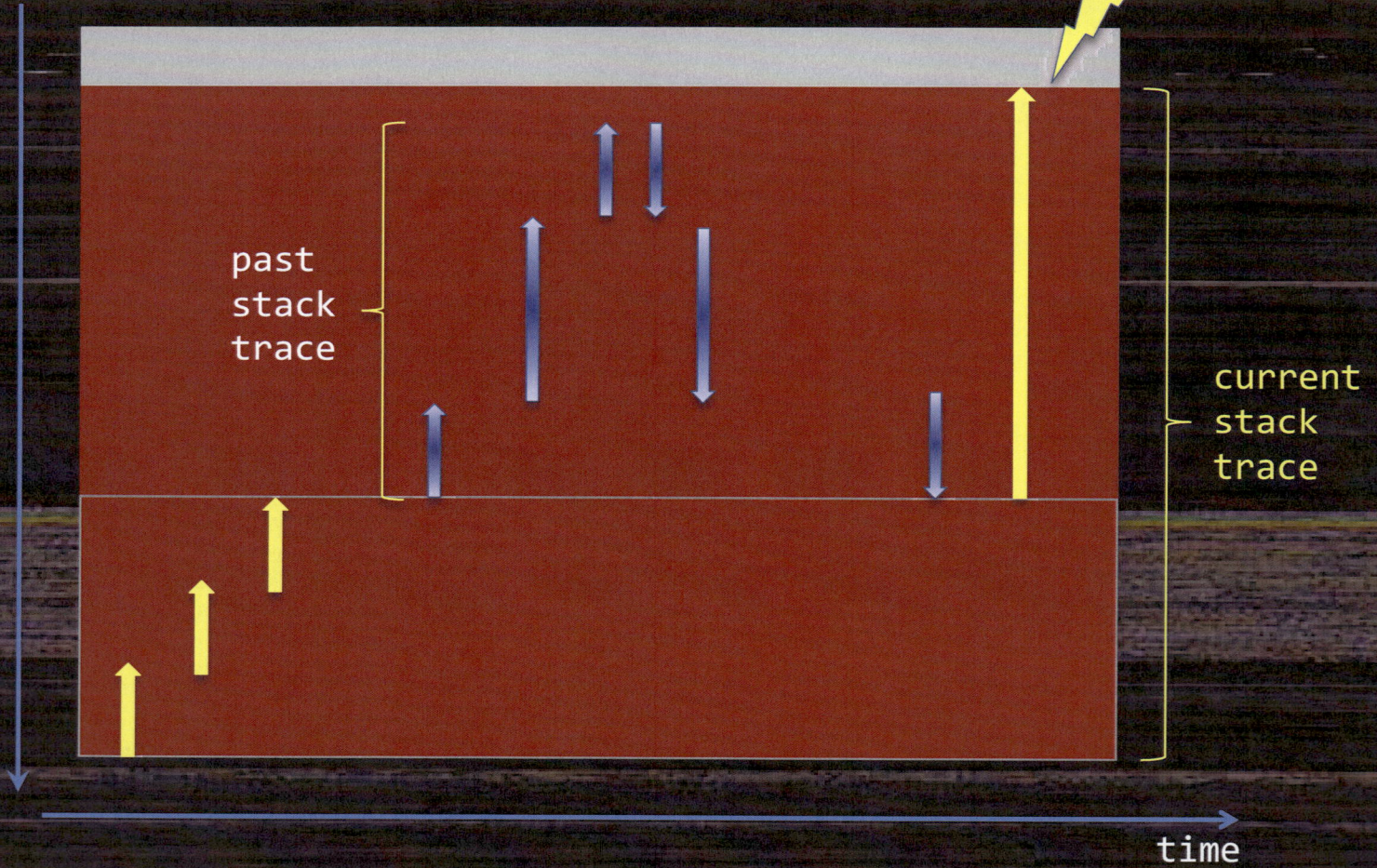

Past Stack Trace

address

past
stack
trace

current
stack
trace

time

© 2013 Software Diagnostics Institute

Example

```
; Current stack trace
0:000> kL
Child-SP          RetAddr           Call Site
[…]
00000000`001af420 00000001`3f6813a9 PastStackTrace!bar_5+0x9
00000000`001af450 00000001`3f681409 PastStackTrace!bar_4+0x39
00000000`001af510 00000001`3f681469 PastStackTrace!bar_3+0x39
00000000`001af5d0 00000001`3f6814c9 PastStackTrace!bar_2+0x39
00000000`001af690 00000001`3f6814f9 PastStackTrace!bar_1+0x39
00000000`001af750 00000001`3f681517 PastStackTrace!bar+0x9
00000000`001af780 00000001`3f6816ec PastStackTrace!main+0x17
00000000`001af7b0 00000000`779f652d PastStackTrace!__tmainCRTStartup+0x144
00000000`001af7f0 00000000`77b2c521 kernel32!BaseThreadInitThunk+0xd
00000000`001af820 00000000`00000000 ntdll!RtlUserThreadStart+0x1d


; Past stack trace
0:000> kL =00000000001ab138
Child-SP          RetAddr           Call Site
[…]
00000000`001ab140 00000001`3f6810b9 PastStackTrace!foo_8+0x49
00000000`001ab200 00000001`3f681119 PastStackTrace!foo_7+0x49
00000000`001ab2c0 00000001`3f681179 PastStackTrace!foo_6+0x49
00000000`001ab380 00000001`3f6811d9 PastStackTrace!foo_5+0x49
00000000`001ab440 00000001`3f681239 PastStackTrace!foo_4+0x49
00000000`001ab500 00000001`3f681299 PastStackTrace!foo_3+0x49
00000000`001ab5c0 00000001`3f6812f9 PastStackTrace!foo_2+0x49
00000000`001ab680 00000001`3f681355 PastStackTrace!foo_1+0x49
00000000`001ab740 00000001`3f681517 PastStackTrace!foo+0x45
00000000`001af780 00000001`3f6816ec PastStackTrace!main+0x17
00000000`001af7b0 00000000`779f652d PastStackTrace!__tmainCRTStartup+0x144
00000000`001af7f0 00000000`77b2c521 kernel32!BaseThreadInitThunk+0xd
00000000`001af820 00000000`00000000 ntdll!RtlUserThreadStart+0x1d
```

© 2013 Software Diagnostics Institute

Further Reading

From Software Diagnostics Library:

Reconstructing Stack Trace Manually

Execution Residue pattern

Incorrect Stack Trace pattern

Truncated Stack Trace pattern

Glued Stack Trace pattern

Debugging TV:

Episode 0xF (Mac OS X)

© 2013 Software Diagnostics Institute

Topics

- Setting guest OS and virtual machine for kernel debugging
- Configuring host WinDbg for kernel debugging
- Examining the guest system
- Simulating a double fault

© 2013 Software Diagnostics Institute

Virtual Machine Setup

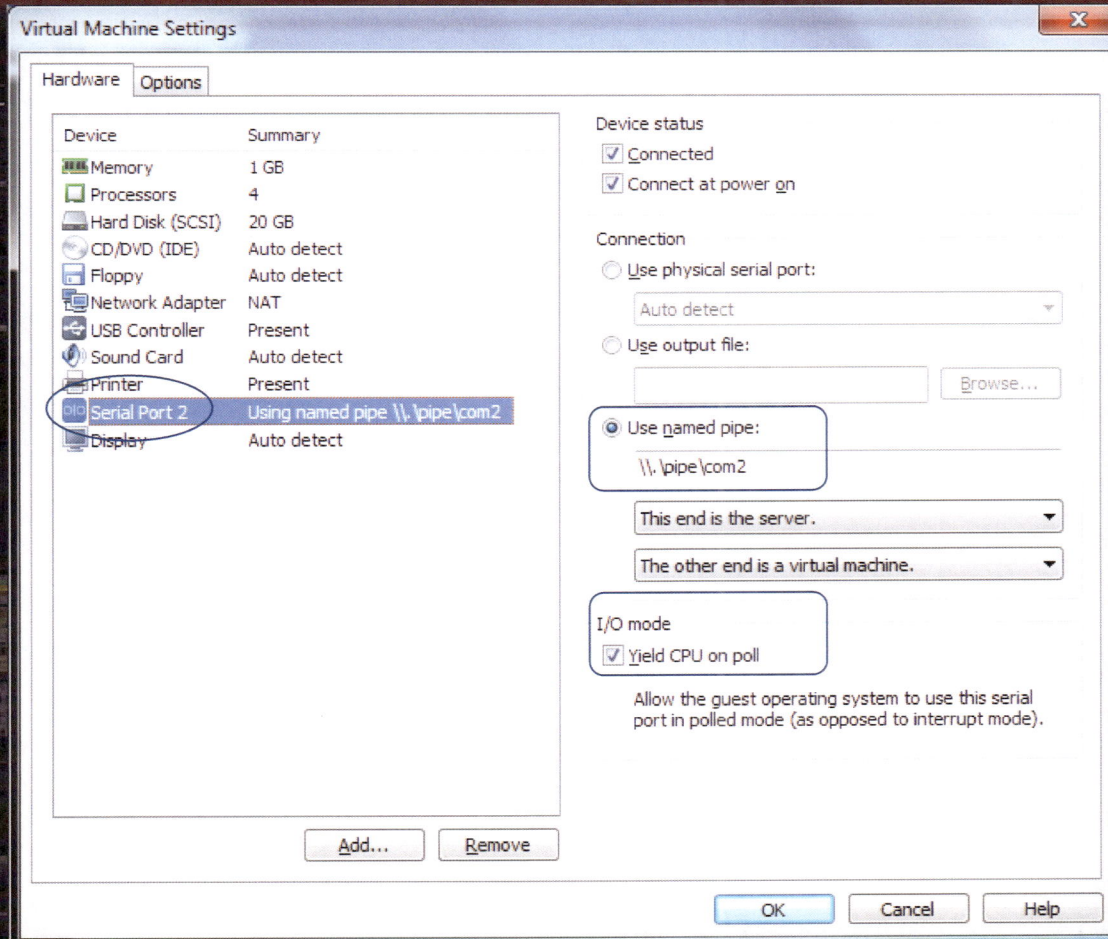

© 2013 Software Diagnostics Institute

Guest OS Setup

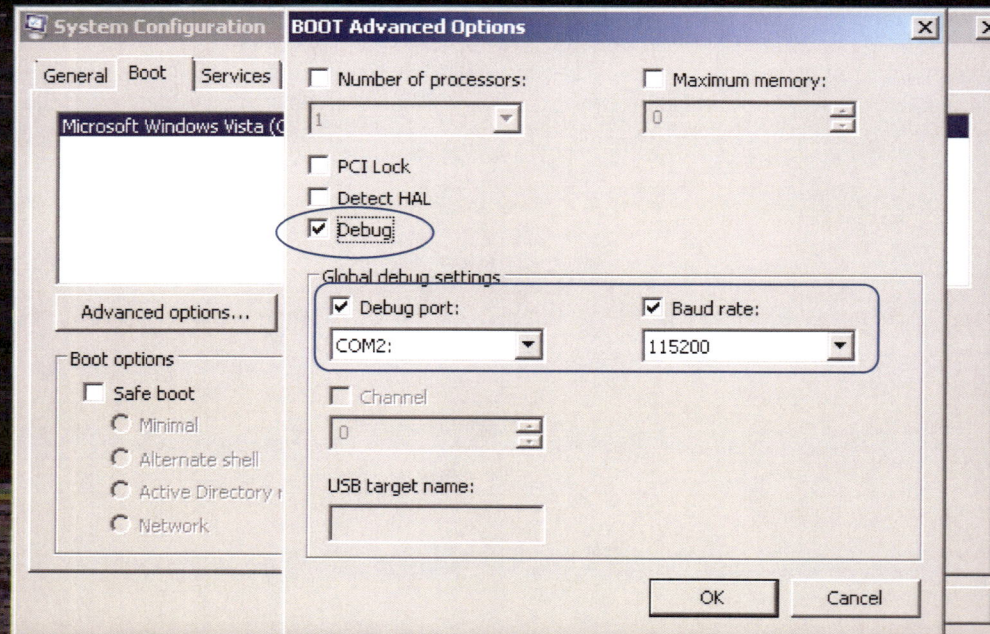

© 2013 Software Diagnostics Institute

Host WinDbg Setup

Kernel Debugging

| COM | 1394 | USB | NET | Local |

Kernel debugging over a COM port or virtual serial device

Baud Rate:
115200

Port:
\\.\pipe\com2

☑ Pipe

☑ Reconnect

Resets:
0

OK   Cancel   Help

© 2013 Software Diagnostics Institute

Double Fault

```
1: kd> k
Child-SP          RetAddr           Call Site
fffff980`00a9e968 fffff800`0184d8f3 nt!KeBugCheckEx
fffff980`00a9e970 fffff800`0184c138 nt!KiBugCheckDispatch+0x73
fffff980`00a9eab0 fffff800`0184b754 nt!KiDoubleFaultAbort+0xb8
fffff980`00ce4f80 fffff800`0184d900 nt!KiDebugTrapOrFault+0x14
fffff980`00ce5118 fffff800`0184b871 nt!KiExceptionDispatch
fffff980`00ce5120 fffff800`0184d900 nt!KiDebugTrapOrFault+0x131
[…]
fffff980`00cea400 fffff800`0184d900 nt!KiDebugTrapOrFault+0x131
fffff980`00cea598 fffff800`0184b871 nt!KiExceptionDispatch
fffff980`00cea5a0 fffff800`0184d900 nt!KiDebugTrapOrFault+0x131
fffff980`00cea738 fffff800`0184b871 nt!KiExceptionDispatch
fffff980`00cea740 fffff800`0184d900 nt!KiDebugTrapOrFault+0x131
fffff980`00cea8d8 fffff800`0184b871 nt!KiExceptionDispatch
fffff980`00cea8e0 fffff800`0184d900 nt!KiDebugTrapOrFault+0x131
fffff980`00ceaa78 fffff800`0184bec3 nt!KiExceptionDispatch
fffff980`00ceaa80 fffff980`13ac910b nt!KiInvalidOpcodeFault+0xc3
fffff980`00ceac10 fffff980`13ac9415 spsys!SPVersion+0x237db
fffff980`00ceac50 fffff980`13ad4e6c spsys!SPVersion+0x23ae5
fffff980`00ceac90 fffff800`01859ca3 spsys!SPVersion+0x2f53c
fffff980`00ceace0 fffff800`01ae1bbb nt!ExpWorkerThread+0x12a
fffff980`00cead50 fffff800`018344f6 nt!PspSystemThreadStartup+0x5b
fffff980`00cead80 00000000`00000000 nt!KxStartSystemThread+0x16
```

© 2013 Software Diagnostics Institute

Topics

- Windows process heap corruption
- Buffer overwrite / overflow
- Buffer underwrite / underflow
- Gflags.exe

© 2013 Software Diagnostics Institute

Overwrite / Overflow

Normal heap

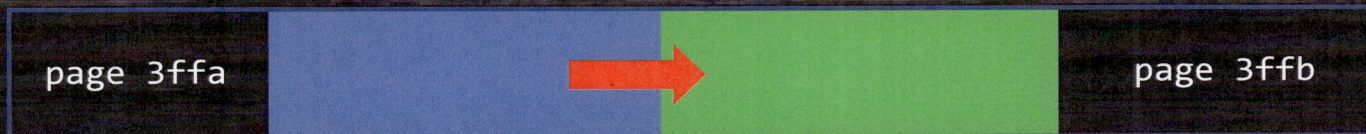

page 3ffa   page 3ffb

Full page heap

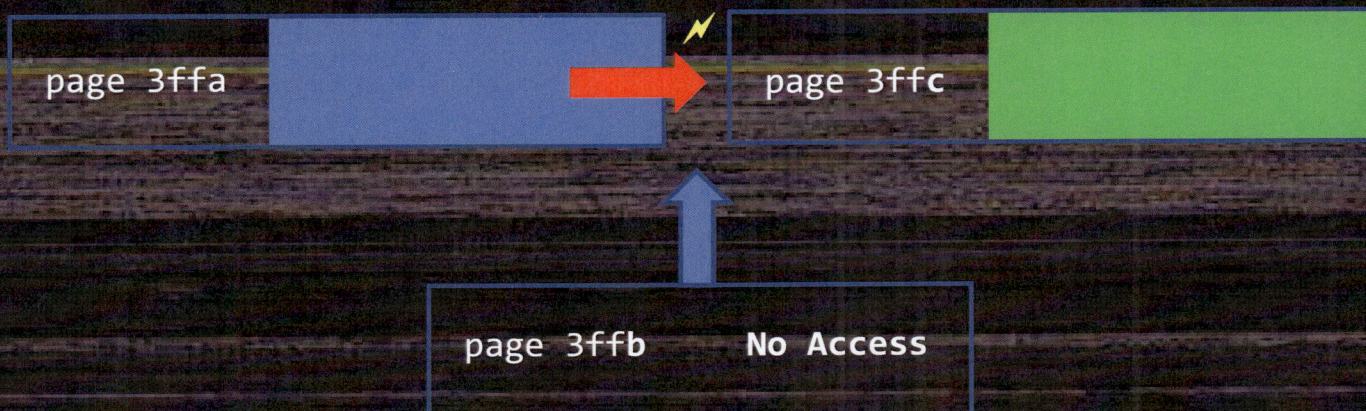

page 3ffa   page 3ffc

page 3ffb   No Access

© 2013 Software Diagnostics Institute

Underwrite / Underflow

Normal heap

page 3ffa   page 3ffb

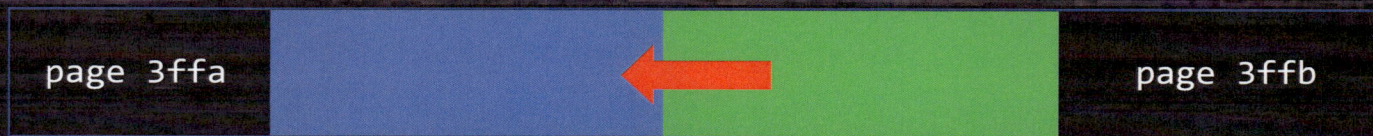

Full page heap

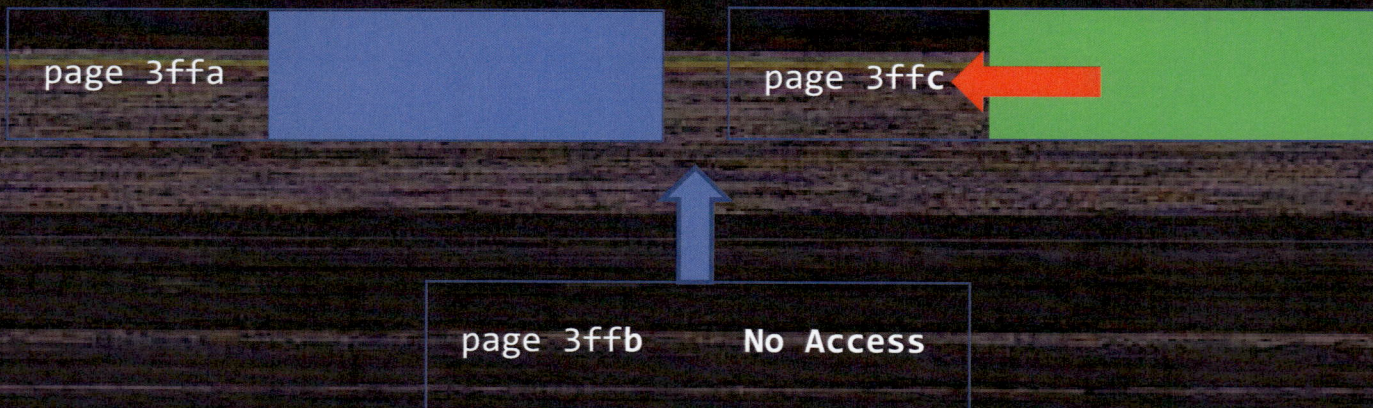

page 3ffa   page 3ffc

page 3ffb   No Access

© 2013 Software Diagnostics Institute

Underwrite / Underflow

Normal heap

page 3ffa   page 3ffb

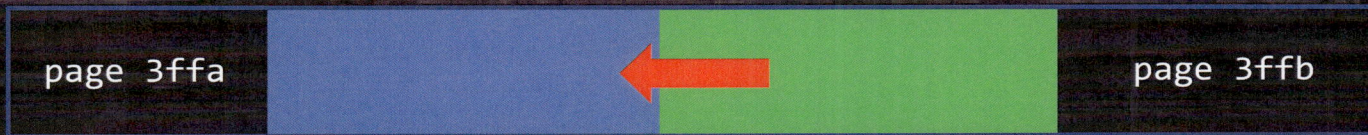

Full page heap (backwards)

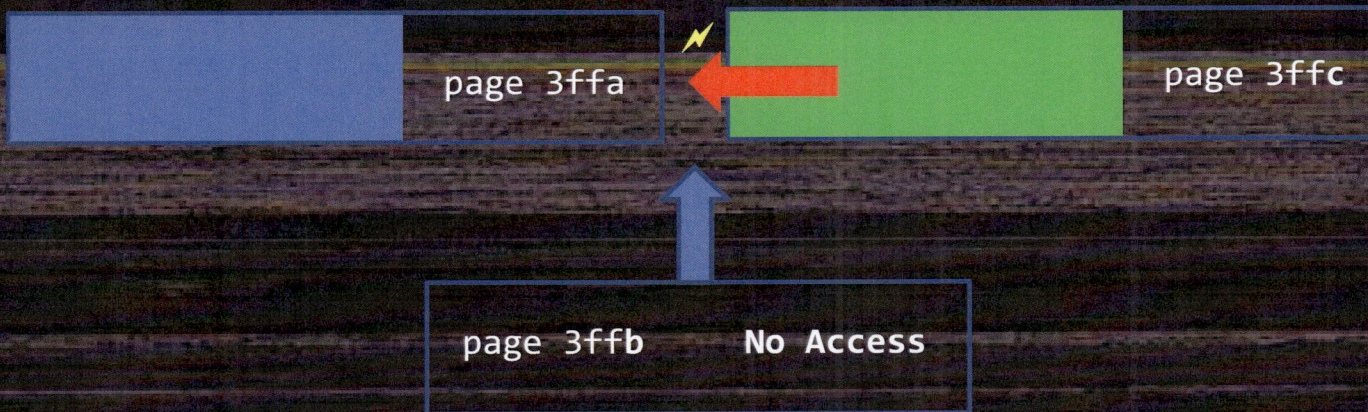

page 3ffa   page 3ffc

page 3ffb   No Access

© 2013 Software Diagnostics Institute

Gflags

Overflow / Overwrite

gflags /p /enable notepad.exe /full

HKEY_LOCAL_MACHINE\SOFTWARE\Microsoft\Windows
NT\CurrentVersion\Image File Execution
Options\notepad.exe

ab (Default)	REG_SZ	(value not set)
ab GlobalFlag	REG_SZ	0x02000000
ab PageHeapFlags	REG_SZ	0x3
011/010 VerifierFlags	REG_DWORD	0x00000001 (1)

Underflow / Underwrite

gflags /p /enable notepad.exe /full /backwards

HKEY_LOCAL_MACHINE\SOFTWARE\Microsoft\Windows
NT\CurrentVersion\Image File Execution
Options\notepad.exe

ab (Default)	REG_SZ	(value not set)
ab GlobalFlag	REG_SZ	0x02000000
ab PageHeapFlags	REG_SZ	0x13
011/010 VerifierFlags	REG_DWORD	0x00000001 (1)

© 2013 Software Diagnostics Institute

Topics

- Modelling Abnormal Software Behaviour
- Disassembling and assembling (x64)
- Pool leak

© 2013 Software Diagnostics Institute

Topics

- Tracing global behaviour
- Example: logging SendMessage API
- Breakpoints with action

© 2013 Software Diagnostics Institute

Sessions and Windows

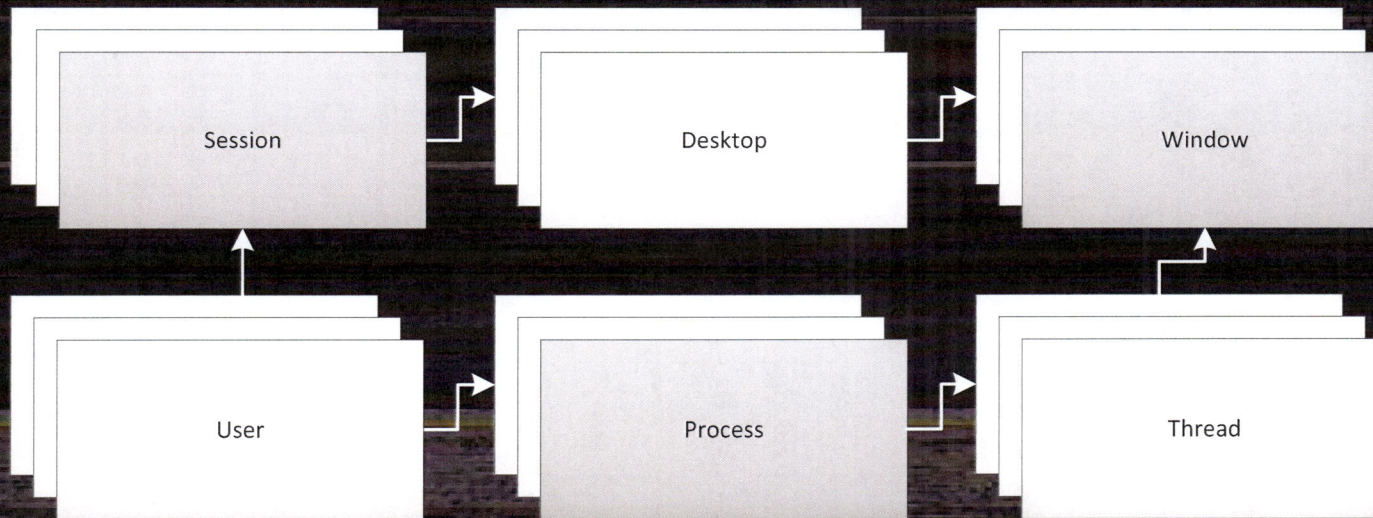

© 2013 Software Diagnostics Institute

Message Hooking

- Spy++
- MessageHistory

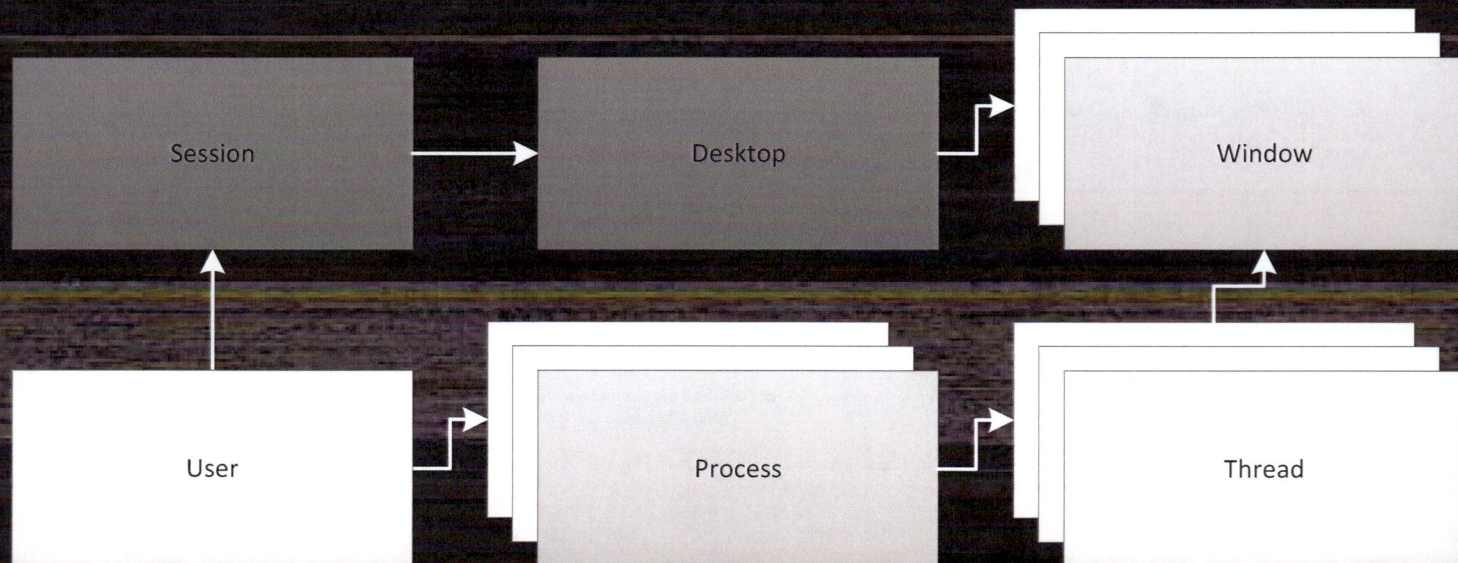

© 2013 Software Diagnostics Institute

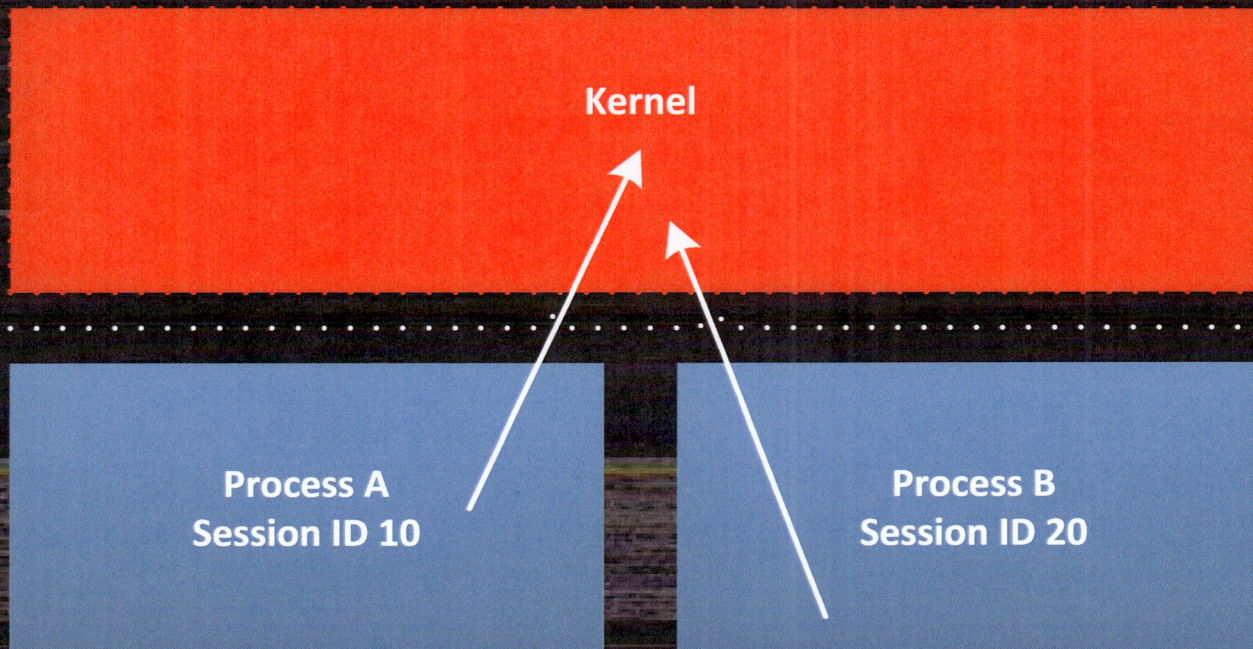

Convergent Point

Kernel

Process A
Session ID 10

Process B
Session ID 20

© 2013 Software Diagnostics Institute

Topics

- Breaking into a process
- Execution history
- Execution residue
- Example

© 2013 Software Diagnostics Institute

Patterns

- Historical Information

- Execution Residue (unmanaged)

- Execution Residue (managed)

© 2013 Software Diagnostics Institute

Topics

- Complete memory dump analysis
- Data recovery: files
- Data recovery: buffers
- Search optimization for x64 dumps

© 2013 Software Diagnostics Institute

Before Blue Screen

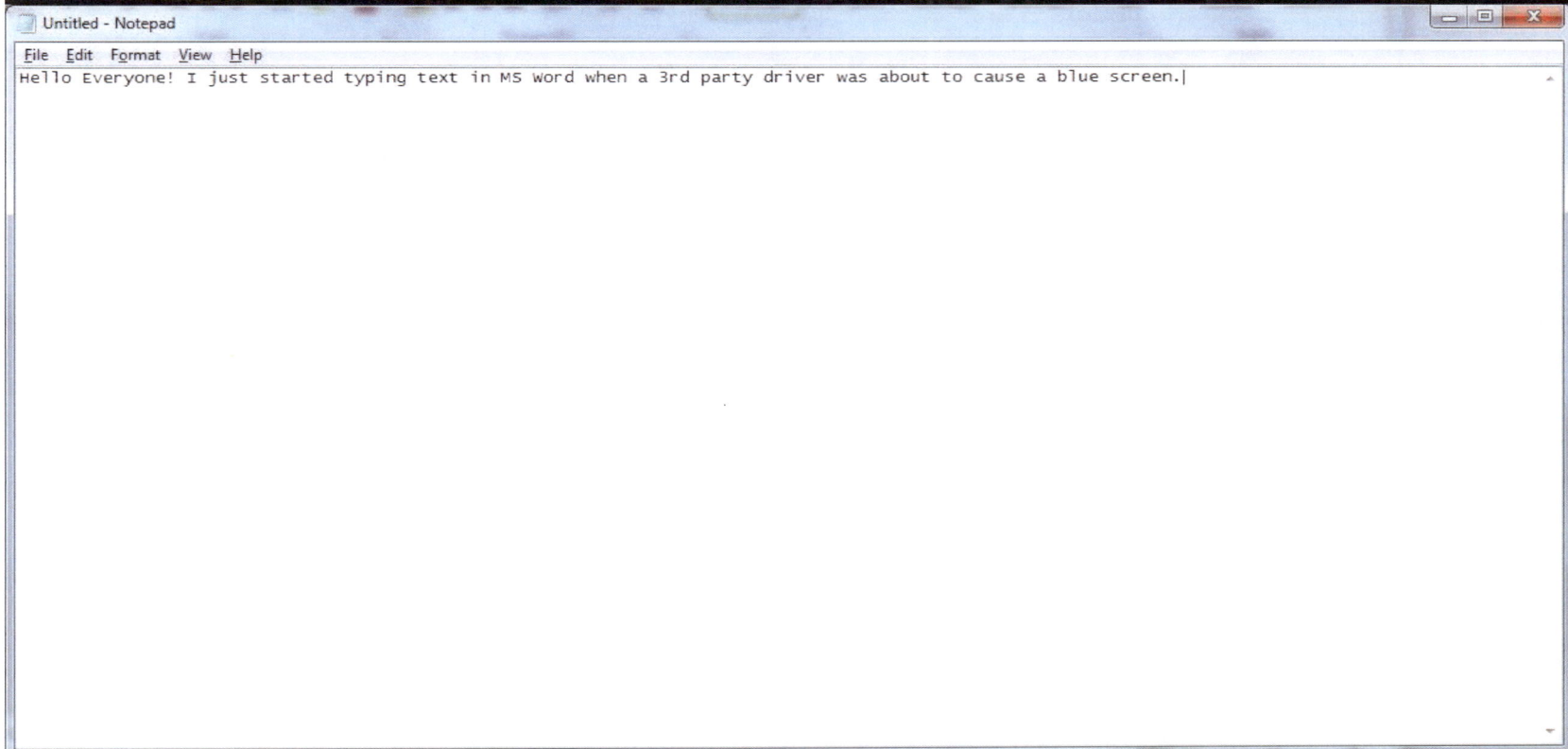

Untitled - Notepad

File Edit Format View Help

Hello Everyone! I just started typing text in MS word when a 3rd party driver was about to cause a blue screen.|

© 2013 Software Diagnostics Institute

Topics

- Heap Leaks: explicit and implicit
- Parameter reconstruction
- Example

© 2013 Software Diagnostics Institute

Varieties of Leaks

- Explicit

    ❖ alloc / missing free

- Implicit

    ❖ API call / missing matching "free" call
    ❖ API call with wrong parameter

© 2013 Software Diagnostics Institute

Modeling

```
void bar(HWND hWnd)
{
    LPCTSTR lpString = L"Hello Weird!";
    int size = 0xFFFFFFF; // "uninitialized" or corrupt

    HDC hDC = GetWindowDC(hWnd);

    if (!TextOut(hDC, 0, 0, lpString, size))
    {
        ReportError(GetLastError());
    }

    ReleaseDC(hWnd, hDC);
}
```

© 2013 Software Diagnostics Institute

Topics

- Trace analysis patterns: Android
- Memory dump analysis patterns
- Stack Trace Collection: Java
- State Dump trace analysis pattern

© 2013 Software Diagnostics Institute

Trace Analysis Patterns

Level	Time	PID	TID	Application	Tag	Text
D	08-26 14:54:5...	161	189		BatterySer...	update start
D	08-26 14:54:5...	161	189		BatterySer...	update start
W	08-26 14:54:5...	161	191		PowerManag...	Timer 0x1->0x0|0x0
I	08-26 14:54:5...	161	191			
E	08-26 14:54:5...	161	190			
D	08-26 14:54:5...	161	191			
D	08-26 14:54:5...	161	191			
D	08-26 14:54:5...	161	191			
I	08-26 14:54:5...	161	191			
V	08-26 14:54:5...	161	191			current orie ↵
D	08-26 14:54:5...	161	194			
D	08-26 14:54:5...	161	194			
D	08-26 14:54:5...	161	194			
D	08-26 14:54:5...	161	194			
I	08-26 14:54:5...	161	190			
W	08-26 14:54:5...	161	190			
W	08-26 14:54:5...	161	190			
D	08-26 14:54:5...	161	190			
V	08-26 14:54:5...	161	191			
D	08-26 14:54:5...	161	194			
D	08-26 14:54:5...	161	194			
D	08-26 14:54:5...	161	194			
D	08-26 14:54:5...	161	194			
D	08-26 14:54:5...	161	194		LockPatter...	getBoolean_three
D	08-26 14:54:5...	161	194		LockPatter...	isSecure() returnfalseUnlockMode =Pattern
V	08-26 14:54:5...	161	194		LockPatter...	**** UPDATE SCREEN: mode=LockScreen last mode=LockScreen
V	08-26 14:54:5...	161	194		LockPatter...	Gone=com.android.internal.policy.impl.PatternUnlockScreen@40a1e8d0
V	08-26 14:54:5...	161	194		LockPatter...	Visible=com.android.internal.policy.impl.LockScreen@4070f198
D	08-26 14:54:5...	7955	7955		PhoneWindow	couldn't save which view has focus because the focused view com.and ↵ roid.internal.policy.impl.PhoneWindow$DecorView@40610898 has no id.
D	08-26 14:54:5...	225	225		FastDormancy	[FD] INTENT ACTION android.intent.action.SCREEN_OFF
D	08-26 14:54:5...	225	225		FastDormancy	[FD] mIsScreenOn: false

Logcat Message Filter Settings

Filter logcat messages by the source's tag, pid or minimum log level.
Empty fields will match all messages.

Filter Name: Telephony

by Log Tag: |

by Log Message:

by PID: 7782

by Application Name:

by Log Level: info ▾

(?)   [OK]   [Cancel]

© 2013 Software Diagnostics Institute

Stack Trace Collection

```java
(new Thread(new Runnable() {
    public void run() {
        while (true)
        {
            try {
                Thread.sleep(5000);
            } catch (InterruptedException e) {
                e.printStackTrace();
            }
            System.out.println("--- Stack Trace Collection ---");
            for (Map.Entry<Thread, StackTraceElement[]> e :
                    Thread.getAllStackTraces().entrySet())
            {
                System.out.println(e.getKey() + ":");
                for (StackTraceElement st : e.getValue())
                    System.out.println("    " + st);
            }
            System.out.println("--- end ---");
        }
    }
})).start();
```

© 2013 Software Diagnostics Institute

State Dump

software trace

Memory Analysis Pattern Catalogue

© 2013 Software Diagnostics Institute

Debugging.TV

Frame 0x33

Presenter: Dmitry Vostokov

SOFTWARE DIAGNOSTICS SERVICES

www.PatternDiagnostics.com

Including Memory Dump and Software Trace Analysis Audit, Seminars,
Certification and Training

Sponsors

OPENTASK
Iterative and Incremental Publishing

Topics

- Spiking Thread pattern (Android)
- Deadlock pattern (Android)
- ADB
- Paratext pattern (Android)

© 2013 Software Diagnostics Institute

Spiking Thread

```
(new Thread(new Runnable() {  // Thread #11
    public void run() {
        while (true) {
            double num = Math.random();
        }
    }
})).start();
```

```
09-08 22:38:54.629: I/System.out(21804): Thread[main,5,main]:
09-08 22:38:54.629: I/System.out(21804):    android.os.MessageQueue.nativePollOnce(Native Method)
09-08 22:38:54.629: I/System.out(21804):    android.os.MessageQueue.next(MessageQueue.java:119)
09-08 22:38:54.629: I/System.out(21804):    android.os.Looper.loop(Looper.java:117)
09-08 22:38:54.629: I/System.out(21804):    android.app.ActivityThread.main(ActivityThread.java:3687)
09-08 22:38:54.639: I/System.out(21804):    java.lang.reflect.Method.invokeNative(Native Method)
09-08 22:38:54.639: I/System.out(21804):    java.lang.reflect.Method.invoke(Method.java:507)
09-08 22:38:54.639: I/System.out(21804):
com.android.internal.os.ZygoteInit$MethodAndArgsCaller.run(ZygoteInit.java:867)
09-08 22:38:54.639: I/System.out(21804):
com.android.internal.os.ZygoteInit.main(ZygoteInit.java:625)
09-08 22:38:54.639: I/System.out(21804):    dalvik.system.NativeStart.main(Native Method)
09-08 20:12:03.779: I/System.out(20147): Thread[Thread-11,5,main]:
09-08 20:12:03.789: I/System.out(20147):    java.util.Random.next(Random.java:90)
09-08 20:12:03.789: I/System.out(20147):    java.util.Random.nextDouble(Random.java:122)
09-08 20:12:03.789: I/System.out(20147):    java.lang.Math.random(Math.java:965)
09-08 20:12:03.789: I/System.out(20147):
com.example.spikingthread.FullscreenActivity$6$1.run(FullscreenActivity.java:150)
09-08 20:12:03.789: I/System.out(20147):    java.lang.Thread.run(Thread.java:1019)
```

© 2013 Software Diagnostics Institute

Deadlock

```java
public void run() {  // Thread #11
    synchronized(cs1) {
        try { Thread.sleep(2000); } catch (InterruptedException e) {}
        synchronized(cs2) {
            try { Thread.sleep(1000); } catch (InterruptedException e) {}
        }
    }
}

public void run() { // Thread #12
    synchronized(cs2) {
        try { Thread.sleep(4000); } catch (InterruptedException e) {}
        synchronized(cs1) {
            try { Thread.sleep(1000); } catch (InterruptedException e) {}
        }
    }
}
```

```
09-08 22:38:54.629: I/System.out(21804): Thread[Thread-11,5,main]:
09-08 22:38:54.629: I/System.out(21804):
com.example.deadlock.FullscreenActivity$6$1.run(FullscreenActivity.java:157)
09-08 22:38:54.629: I/System.out(21804):        java.lang.Thread.run(Thread.java:1019)
09-08 22:38:54.639: I/System.out(21804): Thread[Thread-12,5,main]:
09-08 22:38:54.639: I/System.out(21804):
com.example.deadlock.FullscreenActivity$6$2.run(FullscreenActivity.java:177)
09-08 22:38:54.639: I/System.out(21804):        java.lang.Thread.run(Thread.java:1019)
```

© 2013 Software Diagnostics Institute

Paratext

```
$ ps -t
[...]
app_57     21600 93     146880 19352 ffffffff 00000000 S com.example.spikingthread
app_57     21601 21600  146880 19352 ffffffff 00000000 S HeapWorker
app_57     21602 21600  146880 19352 ffffffff 00000000 S GC
app_57     21603 21600  146880 19352 ffffffff 00000000 S Signal Catcher
app_57     21604 21600  146880 19352 ffffffff 00000000 S JDWP
app_57     21605 21600  146880 19352 ffffffff 00000000 S Compiler
app_57     21606 21600  146880 19352 ffffffff 00000000 S Binder Thread #
app_57     21607 21600  146880 19352 ffffffff 00000000 S Binder Thread #
app_57     21608 21600  146880 19352 ffffffff 00000000 S Thread-10
app_57     21611 21600  146880 19352 ffffffff 00000000 R Thread-11
shell      21619 143    800    336   c00a6fc8 afd0c3bc S /system/bin/sh
root       21631 2      0      0     ffffffff 00000000 S flush-138:13
app_68     21635 93     151092 18456 ffffffff 00000000 S com.example.deadlock
app_68     21636 21635  151092 18456 ffffffff 00000000 S HeapWorker
app_68     21637 21635  151092 18456 ffffffff 00000000 S GC
app_68     21638 21635  151092 18456 ffffffff 00000000 S Signal Catcher
app_68     21639 21635  151092 18456 ffffffff 00000000 S JDWP
app_68     21640 21635  151092 18456 ffffffff 00000000 S Compiler
app_68     21641 21635  151092 18456 ffffffff 00000000 S Binder Thread #
app_68     21642 21635  151092 18456 ffffffff 00000000 S Binder Thread #
app_68     21643 21635  151092 18456 ffffffff 00000000 S Thread-10
app_68     21650 21635  151092 18456 ffffffff 00000000 S Thread-11
app_68     21652 21635  151092 18456 ffffffff 00000000 S Thread-12
[...]
```

© 2013 Software Diagnostics Institute

Debugging.TV

Frame 0x34

Presenter: Dmitry Vostokov

SOFTWARE DIAGNOSTICS SERVICES

www.PatternDiagnostics.com

Including Memory Dump and Software Trace Analysis Audit, Seminars, Certification and Training

Sponsors

OPENTASK
Iterative and Incremental Publishing

Topics

- GDB debugging for Android
- Android processes and threads
- Memory analysis patterns
- Android core dumps

© 2013 Software Diagnostics Institute

Setting Environment

- Remote: GDB Server debugging

- Local: GDB inside Android device

  - Rooted device (Samsung Galaxy Tab 2 7.0, Android 4.2.2)

  - (Eclipse +) Android SDK

  - ADB

  - Dan Drown http://dan.drown.org/android/howto/gdb.html

© 2013 Software Diagnostics Institute

Spiking Thread

```
root@android:/data/local/tmp/bin # ps -t
ps -t
USER      PID   PPID  VSIZE   RSS    WCHAN     PC         NAME
[...]
u0_a33    30703 445   522908  44880  ffffffff  401c6044 S com.example.spikingthread

u0_a33    30707 30703 522908  44880  c00fdc38  401c62a0 S GC
u0_a33    30708 30703 522908  44880  c00ddbc8  401c5b28 S Signal Catcher
u0_a33    30709 30703 522908  44880  c01969c0  401c526c S JDWP
u0_a33    30710 30703 522908  44880  c00fdc38  401c62a0 S Compiler
u0_a33    30711 30703 522908  44880  c00fdc38  401c62a0 S ReferenceQueueD
u0_a33    30712 30703 522908  44880  c00fdc38  401c62a0 S FinalizerDaemon
u0_a33    30713 30703 522908  44880  c00fdc38  401c62a0 S FinalizerWatchd
u0_a33    30714 30703 522908  44880  c0465b2c  401c5148 S Binder_1
u0_a33    30715 30703 522908  44880  c0465b2c  401c5148 S Binder_2
u0_a33    30727 30703 522908  44880  c00fdc38  401c62a0 S Thread-758
u0_a33    30774 30703 522908  44880  00000000  5f54ec08 R Thread-759

root@android:/data/local/tmp/bin # ./gdb --pid=30727
(gdb) bt
bt
#0  0x401c62a0 in __futex_syscall3 () from /system/lib/libc.so
#1  0x401bc580 in __pthread_cond_timedwait_relative ()
   from /system/lib/libc.so

root@android:/data/local/tmp/bin # ./gdb --pid=30774
(gdb) bt
bt
#0  0x5f54e64c in ?? ()
#1  0x5f54e976 in ?? ()
Backtrace stopped: previous frame identical to this frame

(gdb) x/i $pc
x/i $pc
=> 0x5f54e64c:  cbz     r2, 0x5f54e660
```

© 2013 Software Diagnostics Institute

Invalid Pointer

```
Program terminated with signal 11, Segmentation fault.
#0  0x40128be2 in ?? () from /system/lib/libc.so

(gdb) bt
bt
#0  0x40128be2 in ?? () from /system/lib/libc.so
#1  0x4012c54c in _fwalk () from /system/lib/libc.so
#2  0x4012c54c in _fwalk () from /system/lib/libc.so
Backtrace stopped: previous frame identical to this frame

(gdb) info r
info r
r0              0x27        39
r1              0xdeadbaad          3735927469
r2              0x40159258          1075155544
r3              0x0         0
r4              0x0         0
r5              0xbe9ff564          3198154084
r6              0x32542c 3298348
r7              0x648    1608
r8              0x8682f0 8815344
r9              0x1         1
r10             0x93b2d8 9679576
r11             0xbe9ff6c4          3198154436
r12             0x323010 3289104
sp              0xbe9ff560          0xbe9ff560
lr              0x4012c54d          1074971981
pc              0x40128be2          0x40128be2
fps             0x0         0
cpsr            0x60000030          1610612784

(gdb) x/i $pc
x/i $pc
=> 0x40128be2:   strb    r0, [r1, #0]
```

© 2013 Software Diagnostics Institute

Debugging.TV

http://www.youtube.com/DebuggingTV

!Ad Hardcore Software Diagnostics Training

Accelerated Windows Memory Dump Analysis

Accelerated Linux Core Dump Analysis

© 2021 Software Diagnostics Institute

www.ingramcontent.com/pod-product-compliance
Lightning Source LLC
Chambersburg PA
CBRC091409210326
41598CB00014BA/875

9 781912 636860